THE GEOGRAPHICAL HISTORY

OF AMERICA

OR

THE RELATION OF HUMAN NATURE

TO THE HUMAN MIND

1

WHEN Gertrude Stein was a young girl, the twentieth century was approaching like a distant train whose hoot you could only just hear. A whole age was about to end. Nations would rededicate themselves, an entire generation bite into a fresh loaf, turn over a new leaf . . . tremble, pray. Despite this threat from the realm of number, though, most of the world went on as before, repeating itself over and over in every place, beginning and rebeginning, again and again and again.

Kipling had just written *The Phantom Rickshaw*. Stevenson was about to bring out *The Master of Ballantrae*, Howells to publish *A Hazard of New Fortunes*, while recently young Miss Stein had composed a melodrama called *Snatched from Death, or the Sundered Sisters*.

Henry James had also been busy. *The Bostonians* and *The Princess Casamassima* appeared in the same year, almost moments ago, it must have seemed, and *Scribner's Magazine* was now serializing *A London Life*. Writing machines were prominently advertised in the same periodical, as well as a restorative medicine made of cocainized beef, wine, and iron, said to be invaluable for nervous prostration, brain exhaustion, cases of the opium, tobacco, alcohol or chloral habit, gastric catarrh, and weak states of the voice or generative systems, among other things. Indeed, women were frequently in need of similar elixirs to combat depressions of the spirit, neurasthenia, sick headache, dyspepsia, and loss of appetite. Adelina Patti was recommending Pears Soap. There were several new developments among stoves. Lew Wallace, Dr. Abbott, Motley's *Works*, Walter Besant's novels, Charles Dudley Warner, Rider Haggard, and a series labeled "The English Men of Letters" were being smartly puffed, as well as the stories of Constance Fenimore Woolson and an edifying volume by Charles Reade called *Bible Characters* (12 mo, cloth, 75 cents).

At Gettysburg, on the twenty-fifth anniversary of the battle, George Parsons Lathrop read a very long commemorative ode.

> And, with a movement magnificent,
> Pickett, the golden-haired leader,
> Thousands and thousands flings onward, as if he sent
> Merely a meek interceder.

And at the great Paris Exposition, among the Americans represented, Thomas Hovenden showed his picture, *The Last Moments of John Brown*, of which

one critic said: "It is easy to believe that we are looking at a faithful transcript of the actual scene, and that
photography itself could not have made a more
accurate record." "It is the best American painting yet
produced," wrote another. Holloway's reading stand
was deemed particularly good for ladies, combining a
book rest, dictionary holder, lamp stand, and invalid's
table. It was sold where made in Cuyahoga Falls,
Ohio.

For some time Gertrude Stein had been absorbed,
she claimed, in Shakespeare (of course), and in
Wordsworth (the long dull late and densely moral
poems particularly), Scott's wonderful *Waverley*,
Burns, Bunyan, Crabbe, in Carlyle's *Frederick the
Great*, Fielding, Smollett, and even Lecky's formid-
able *Constitutional History of England*—works of the
sort I'd cite, too, if I were asked. Prognostications of
doom were also common, and increasing. Arks were
readied, mountaintops sought out. Number for some
was still number: a mark on a tube was magical . . .
a circled day . . . a scratch on a tree . . . layer in a
rock. The International Date Line runs like a wall
through the ocean.

We can only guess whether the calendar had any
influence on her, although later no one was to
champion the new century more wholeheartedly, or
attempt to identify America with modernity. The
United States was the oldest country in the world, she

said, because it had been in the twentieth century longer. In any case, Gertrude Stein, at age fifteen, thought frequently of death and change and time. Young girls can. She did not think about dying, which is disagreeable, even to young girls, but about death, which is luxurious, like a hot soak. The thought would appear as suddenly as moist grass in the morning, very gently, often after reading, on long reflective walks; and although it distressed her to think that there were civilizations which had perished altogether, she applauded the approaching turn. It was mostly a matter of making room. "I was there to begin to kill what was not dead, the nineteenth century which was so sure of evolution and prayers, and esperanto and their ideas," she said. It would be a closing, as the opening of puberty had been. A lid. Her own ending, even, did not disturb her. Dissolution did—coming apart at the seams—and she had, as many do, early fears of madness, especially after reading *The Cenci* or attending a performance of *Dr. Jekyll and Mr. Hyde.* She held little orgies of eating, liked to think and read of revolutions, imagined cruelties. She consumed anything, everything, as we have seen, and then complained that there was "Nothing but myself to feed my own eager self, nothing given to me but musty books."

Scribner's Magazine was serializing *A London Life.*

It contained plot, customs, characters, moral issues, insight, endless analysis, a little description, and went over its chosen ground often like an elephant in mittens. There was another of those essays on the decline of the drama in a recent *Harper's*. This one was quite decent really, by Brander Matthews, and in it he argued that one reason for the apparent death of the drama was the life of the novel—the present art form of the public—in particular, the immense early success of Scott's *Waverley* novels. *Scribner's* July issue of 1888 catches up *A London Life* at the beginning of Chapter V:

"And are you telling me the perfect truth when you say that Captain Crispin was not there?"

"The perfect truth?" Mrs. Berrington straightened herself to her height, threw back her head and measured her interlocutress up and down; this was one of the many ways in which it is to be surmised that she knew she looked very handsome indeed. Her interlocutress was her sister, and even in a discussion with a person long since under the charm she was not incapable of feeling that her beauty was a new advantage.

In "Composition as Explanation" Gertrude Stein would argue that between generations and over time, the "only thing different . . . is what is seen and what is seen depends upon how everybody is doing everything." "Everything is the same except composition."

She became, as she grew, increasingly unsure of who she was, a situation now so normal among the younger members of the middle class as to seem an inevitable part of middle-human development, like awkwardness and acne. Gertrude was a bit of a gawk already, aloof, cool, heavy, more and more alone. Her mother was an ineffectual invalid, gradually draining in her bed until, even before she died, she was emptied out of the world. Her father was a nuisance: stocky, determined, uneducated, domineering, quarrelsome, ambitious, notional, stern. When she was seventeen her father died, and "then our life without a father began a very pleasant one."

Chapter V. In the old books there were chapters and verses, sections, volumes, scenes, parts, lines, divisions which had originated with the Scriptures ("chapter," for instance, a word for the head like *tête* and "title"); there were sentences, paragraphs, and numbered pages to measure the beat of each heart, the course of a life, every inference of reason, and the march, as they say, of time. But the present was the only place we were alive, and the present was like a painting, without before or after, spread to be sure, but not in time; and although, as William James had proved, the present was not absolutely flat, it was nevertheless not much thicker than pigment. Geography would be the study appropriate to it: mapping body space. The earth might be round but experience, in effect, was flat. Life might be long but living was as brief as each breath in breathing. Without a past, in the prolonged narrowness of any "now," wasn't everything in a constant condition of commencement? Then, too, breathing is repeating—it is beginning and re-beginning, over and over, again and again and again.

What is the breath-before-last worth?

The youngest, she had been pampered as a baby, and she took care to be pampered all her life. "Little Gertie," her father once wrote, "is a little schnatterer. She talks all day long and so plainly. *She outdoes them all.* She's such a round little pudding, toddles around the whole day and repeats everything that's said or done." Yet she became, as she grew, increasingly unsure of who she was. Her eldest brother, soon off to college and career, seemed distant in his age, while the next, named Simon, she thought simple—as, indeed, he was. "My sister four years older simply existed for me because I had to sleep in the same room with her. It is natural not to care about a sister, certainly not when she is four years older and grinds her teeth at night."

She loved her brother, Leo, but she had no trust of men. It becomes a central theme. "Menace" was the word they went around in. Still, she and Leo were invariably "two together two," although Leo always led, and when Leo went to Harvard, Gertrude later came to Radcliffe, and when Leo began to study biology at Johns Hopkins, Gertrude enrolled in medicine there, and when her brother went to Italy finally, she soon abandoned her studies to join him. They were together for a while in London, shared a flat in Paris, gathered paintings almost by not moving, like dust.

She shared something else with this brother, something deeply significant, something fundamental: an accidental life. When they thought about it, Gertrude said, it made them feel funny. The Steins had planned on having five children, and then, efficiently, had had them. However, two of these children died soon enough so they never "counted," and this made room for Leo, first, and then for Gertrude, so that when, at the beginning of this book, she writes: "If nobody had to die how would there be room enough for any of us who now live to have lived," she is not merely paraphrasing Hume's famous reply to Boswell who, as the philosopher lay becalmed on his deathbed, injudiciously asked if it was not possible that there might be a future state: "It is also possible that a piece of coal put on the fire will not burn," Hume answered, meanly remaining in the realm of matter. "That men should exist forever is a most unreasonable fancy . . .

The trash of every age must then be preserved and new Universes must be created to contain such infinite numbers."

I do not believe she had any knowledge of Frederick Jackson Turner's frontier hypothesis, but her understanding of American history was based on something very like it: "In the United States there is more space where nobody is than where anybody is." There is no question that she, like Turner, thought human behavior was in great part a function of the amount of free land available. On the frontier, Turner believed, civilization was regularly being reborn. When westward the course of empire no longer took its way, Americans moved "in" and went east to Paris in order to go west within the mind—a land like their own without time. And Gertrude Stein believed Americans were readier than Europeans, consequently, to be the new cultural pioneers. The mind . . . The human mind went on like the prairie, on and on without limit.

It is characteristic of her method here and elsewhere that every general thought find exact expression in the language of her own life; that every general thought in fact be the outcome of a repeated consideration of solidly concrete cases—both wholly particular and thoroughly personal—and further, that these occasions be examined, always, in the precise form of their original occurrence; in which, then, they continue to be contained as if they were parts of a sacred text that cannot be tampered with substantially, only slightly rearranged, as a musician might lengthen the vowels or repeat the words of a lyric to compose a song, skip a little now and then, or call for an extensive reprise. "I was there to begin to kill what was not dead . . ."

And what is Mrs. Berrington doing as we come to the end of this month's episode?

"Where are you going—where are you going—where are you going?" Laura broke out.

The carriages moved on, to set them down, and while the footman was getting off the box Selina said: "I don't pretend to be better than other women, but you do!" And being on the side of the house, she quickly stepped out and carried her crowned brilliancy through the long-lingering daylight and into the open portals.

(To be continued.)

Much must go, however good, for Gertrude Stein to be. Much of Gertrude Stein would have to be subtracted once she discovered who she was.

Born in Allegheny, Pennsylvania. It does seem unlikely, but in American letters the unlikely is not unusual: Hart Crane came from Garretsville, Ohio; Pound was born in Idaho; neither Michigan nor

Mississippi have any prima facie promise; Wallace Stevens saw exquisite light in Reading; Katherine. Anne Porter in Indian Creek, Texas; Edward Arlington Robinson in Tide Head, Maine; and for T. S. Eliot even St. Louis is odd. They mostly moved anyway. Who thinks of Robert Frost as a tike in San Francisco? And the Steins left almost immediately for Vienna, where her father hoped that family connections there might help him in his wool business. He really did write back that little Gertie "toddles around the whole day and repeats everything that's said and done." After a period in Paris, the Steins returned to Baltimore, but soon they swapped houses, climates, coasts again, and crossed the country to live in Oakland, California, where Gertrude's father became successfully connected with, for god's sake, a cable railway company.

Hoist up a hill. And with certain exceptions modern American writing has been overwhelmed by space: rootlessness, we often say, that's our illness, and we are right; we're sick of changing house, of moving, of cutting loose, of living in vans and riding cycles, of using up and getting on (that's how we age), until sometimes one feels there's nothing but geography in this country, and certainly a geographical history is the only kind it can significantly have; so that the strange thing is that generally those years which both

Freud and the Roman Catholic Church find crucial
to our character are seldom connected to the trunk,
except perhaps as decals: ·memorials of Mammoth
Cave, ads for Herold's Club. Well, what's the point of
being born in Oak Park if you're going to kill yourself
in Ketchum? Our history simply became "the West"
where time and life went. So what's the point in St.
Paul if you are going to die in Hollywood of an
alcoholic heart? Like Henry James we developed an
enlarged sense of locale, but we were tourists. And
Gertrude Stein lived in hotels, ships, trains, rented
rooms, at aunts', with friends, in flats, with chums, and
grew up with her books, her body, and her brother—
nothing more, and no one else.

Of course, you could say that democracies have
never had a history; that they cannot run in place;
they must expand; they must have space. In New
England, in the South, life went sometimes in another
direction, and it was, naturally enough, one of the
lures of Europe: to be in the presence of people who
had lived for a long time alongside things and other
people who had been allowed to live for a long time
alongside them; consequently to observe objects and
relations come into being, alter, age, fade, disappear,
and to see that process rather constantly; to feel in
things one's own use of them—like old clothes, maybe,
streets, shops, castles, churches, mills—as one's own

person felt one's self—in hills, paths, lakes, fields, creeks—since we seldom gawk at our own changes as though passing by on a bus, but learn to live them with the unconscious ease which daily life and custom gradually confer, like the wear of water and the growth of grass; still Gertrude Stein blew "the American trumpet as though it were the whole of Sousa's band" and always spoke European brokenly; she was perhaps the last of our serious writers to, in the square sense, love her country, and she moved her writing even through her own enthusiasms (Henry James and Richardson and Eliot), as painfully as through a thicket, straight into the present where it became, in every sense of this she understood, "American" and "measureless."

But not in a moment was this accomplished. In a life. The resolution required would be heroic. Shortly after she began living in Paris with her brother, she completed a manuscript which was not published for nearly fifty years: a curiously wooden work of relentless and mostly tiresome psychological analysis which she called, with crushing candor, *Quod Erat Demonstrandum*. However, in this brief novel about the personal relationships between three depersonalized paper women, plotted as a triangle on which the lines are traveled like a tramway, the points incessantly intersected—in which, though much is shown, nothing's proved, and everyone is exhausted—Gertrude Stein's sexual problem surfaces. Clearly, she has had a kind of love affair with another woman. Clearly, too, the circumstances of her life were now combining against her, compelling her to rely more and more upon a self she did not have. She lacked a locale which might help to define her and a family she could in general accept; she had grown into a hulksome female and become a bluestocking, yet she remained professionless and idle; in fact, she was a follower at present, fruit fly, gnat, silent in front of Leo while he lectured to their friends on his latest fads and finds; she was a faithless Jew, a coupon clipper, exile anyhow, and in addition, she was desperately uncertain of her own sexuality. The problem of personal identity, which is triumphantly overcome in *The Geographical History*, would occupy her henceforth, particularly in the most ambitious work of her career, *The Making of Americans*.

Furthermore her brother was beginning to ridicule her writing.

Still she listened to Leo; she looked at Cézanne; she translated Flaubert; and this subordination of ear, eye, and mind, eventually released her, because Flaubert and Cézanne taught the same lesson; and as she examined the master's portrait of his wife, she realized that the reality of the model had been superseded by the reality of the composition. Everything in the painting was related to everything else in the painting, and to everything else equally (there were no lesser marks or moments), while the relation of any line or area of color in the painting to anything outside the painting (to a person in this case) was accidental, superfluous, illusory. The picture was of Mme. Cézanne. It had been painted by her husband. It was owned by the Steins. Thus the picture had an *identity*. But the painting was an *entity*. So a breast was no more important than a button, gray patch or green line. Breasts might be more important than buttons to a vulgar observer, but in biology, where a mouse and a man were equal, in art, in our experience of how things are presented to us in any present moment, in mathematics—indeed, in any real whole or well-ordered system—there was a wonderful and democratic equality of value and function. There was, she said, no "up" in American religion either, no hierarchy, no ranking of dominions and powers.

Identities were what you needed to cash a check or pass a border guard. Identities had neighbors, relatives, husbands, and wives. Pictures were similarly authenticated. Poems were signed. Identities were the persons hired, the books and buildings bought and sold, the famous "things," the stars. She drew the distinction very early. In *The Geographical History* she would describe it as the difference between human nature and the human mind.

Gertrude Stein liked to begin things in February. Henry James has written *The Golden Bowl* and it will take a war to end the century. Never mind. Although the novel as it had been known was now complete, and she has meanwhile doubled her fifteen years without appreciable effect, still there was in what was being written (*Nostromo*, last year; *The House of Mirth*, just out; and *The Man of Property*, forthcoming), for instance, that socially elevated tone, the orotund authorial voice, the elegant drawing-room diction, that multitude of unfunctional details like flour to thicken gravy; there were those gratuitous posturings, nonsensical descriptions, empty conversations, hollow plots, both romance and Grub Street realism; and there so often remained the necessity, as Howells complained, to write with the printer at one's heels, therefore the need to employ suspense like a drunken chauffeur, Chapter Vs and other temporal divisions as though the author commanded an army, and all of the rest of the paraphernalia required by serialization and the monthly purchase of magazines.

She saw how the life of the model had been conferred upon the portrait. And in the central story of *Three Lives* (they were still stories), she captured the feeling she wanted in words.

All that long day, with the warm moist young spring stirring in him, Jeff Campbell worked, and thought, and beat his breast, and wandered, and spoke aloud, and was silent, and was certain, and then in doubt and then keen to surely feel, and then all sodden in him; and he walked, and he sometimes ran fast to lose himself in his rushing, and he bit his nails to pain and bleeding, and he tore his hair so that he could be sure he was really feeling, and he never could know what it was right, he now should be doing.

The rhythms, the rhymes, the heavy monosyllabic beat, the skillful rearrangements of normal order, the carefully controlled pace, the running on, the simplicity, exactness, the passion . . . in the history of language no one had written like this before, and the result was as striking in its way, and as successful, as *Ulysses* was to be.

Neither *Three Lives* nor *The Making of Americans* eliminated the traditional novel's endless, morally motivated, psychological analyses, though she would manage that eventually. *A Long Gay Book* was begun as another investigation of the relationships between people, in this case mainly pairs, but it gradually wandered from that path into pure song. "I sing," she said, "and I sing and the tunes I sing are what are tunes if they come and I sing. I sing I sing." For instance:

Wet weather, wet pen, a black old tiger skin, a shut in shout and a negro coin and the best behind and the sun to shine.

She was readying herself for *Tender Buttons*. But what would never disappear from her work, despite her revolutionary zeal, was her natural American bent toward self-proclamation and her restless quest for truth—especially that, because it would cause her to render some aspects of reality with a ruthlessness rare in any writer, and at a greater risk to her art than most.

Alice Toklas came to live, to type, to correct the proof of *Three Lives*, which Gertrude was printing at her own expense, to manage, companion, cook, protect, while Leo at last left to fulfill his promise as a failure, taking the Matisses and the Renoirs with him, and allowing his sister finally her leeway, her chance to define herself, which she firmly, over decades, did: as an eccentric, dilettante, and gossip, madwoman, patron, genius, tutor, fraud, and queer—the Mother Goose of Montparnasse.

I write for myself and strangers. It took many years; she had to bring out most of her books herself; usually they appeared long after they'd been written, in silence, to indifference, incomprehension, jeers; but in time there were too many strangers: curiosity seekers, sycophants, opportunists, disciples. She hugely enjoyed her growing celebrity, but she noticed what she thought was a change in herself, and she began, vaguely, to be alarmed. In 1933 *The Autobiography of Alice B. Toklas* was published in the U.S.A. with great success, portions of it appearing in *The Atlantic Monthly.* Suddenly there was money she had earned. *Three Lives* went into The Modern Library. She was nearing sixty, 4 × her 15 yrs. It seemed like a good time to go back.

Gertrude Stein would return to the United States like a lion, she said, and word of her arrival did run in lights around the Times Building, reporters met her boat and filled twelve columns of the city papers with news and mostly friendly comment about her.

. . . we saw an electric sign moving around a building and it said Gertrude Stein has come and that was upsetting . . . I like it to happen . . . but always it does give me a little shock of recognition and non-recognition. It is one of the things most worrying in the subject of identity.

She had come home but, although she was recognized in the streets of New York by strangers, she could not find again the San Francisco of her childhood.

. . . it was frightening quite frightening driving there and on top of Nob Hill where we were to stay, of course it had not been like that and yet it was like that, Alice Toklas found it natural but for me it was a trouble yes it was . . .

Along with the face of Gracie Allen, she was caricatured by Covarrubias in *Vogue*; in Chicago she had a chance to see her own *Four Saints in Three Acts*; at Princeton police were used to hold back the crowd which came to hear her lecture. "Americans really want to make you happy." And she would plunge into traffic with a child's trusting unconcern. "All these people, including the nice taxi drivers, recognize and are careful of me."

Queerly companioned and oddly dressed, deep-voiced, direct, she loved being a celebrity and was consequently charming, her autograph was sought, and she and Alice met old friends, publishers, passers-by and tradesmen, students, journalists, teachers, many who were rich and famous from all parts of a country they were both seeing from the air for the first time, the mountains subsiding like a fountain, the desert like a waterless floor of the sea, the whole land lying in lines which Masson, Braque, or Picasso might have drawn. She saw the same flatness, after so much European brick and tile, in the wooden buildings of America, but it was the map in the air which delighted her most because it taught her what the human mind was capable of: flying without wings, seeing without eyes, knowing without evident data. Yet in East Oakland, on the shabby streets where she had played as a child, experience proved empty. What is the point of being born a little girl if you are going to grow up to be a man?

Back in France she tried to digest the lessons of her fame. A woman and artist who had been for much of her life without self or audience, she now had both, but what, after all, did it come to—this self she was famous for? In *Vogue's* "Impossible Interview," Gracie Allen is made to say: "Now Gertie, don't you start to make sense, or people will begin to understand you, and then you won't mean anything at all." These reporters, followers, and friends—they were merely hearts that spaniel'd her at heels . . . She'd looked back, snuffled at her roots, found, seen, felt, nothing.

The Geographical History of America is a culminating work, though not the outcome of her meditations. Those she summed up in an essay, "What Are Masterpieces?" written a year later. This book is the stylized presentation of the process of meditation itself, with many critical asides. In the manner of her earliest piece, *Q.E.D.*, it demonstrates far more than it proves, and although it is in no sense a volume of philosophy (Gertrude Stein never "argues" anything) , it is, philosophically, the most important of her texts. She very much wanted Thornton Wilder to write an extended commentary to accompany it, but she had to settle finally for the graceful introduction which is reprinted here. If we follow her thought as Theseus did the thread of Ariadne, I think we find at the end the justice, if not the total truth, of her boast that the most serious thinking about the nature of literature in the twentieth century has been done by a woman.

2

Life is repetition, and in a dozen different ways Gertrude Stein set out to render it. We have only to think how we pass our days: the doorbell rings, the telephone, sirens in the street, steps on the stairs, the recurrent sounds of buzzers, birds, and vacuum cleaners; then as we listen we suck our teeth; those are our feet approaching, so characteristic the tread can be identified, and that's our little mew of annoyance at the interruption, too, as well as the nervous look which penetrates the glass, the fumble with the latch, the thought: I must remember to oil this lock; whereupon we are confronted by a strange man who is nevertheless saying something totally familiar about brooms. Suppose he is truly a stranger. Still, we have seen salesmen before, men before, brooms; the accent is familiar, the tone, the tie, the crooked smile, the pity we are asked for, the submissive shoulders, yet the vague threat in the forward foot, the extended palm like the paw of a begging bear. Everything, to the last detail, is composed of elements we have already experienced a thousand and a thousand thousand times. Even those once-in-a-lifetime things—overturning a canoe in white water or being shot at, pursuing a squirrel through the attic, sexual excess—are merely unusual combinations of what has been repeatedly around. Our personal habits express it, laws of nature predict it, genes direct it, the edicts of the state encourage or require it, universals sum it up.

The range of our sensations, our thoughts, our feelings, is generally fixed, and so is our experience of relations. Make an analysis, draw up a list. Life is rearrangement, and in a dozen different ways Gertrude Stein set out to render it. We are not clocks, designed to repeat without remainder, to mean nothing by a tick, not even the coming tock, and so we must distinguish between merely mechanical repetition, in which there is no progress of idea, no advance or piling up of wealth, and that which seriously defines our nature, describes the central rhythms of our lives.

Almost at once she realized that language itself is a complete analogue of experience because it, too, is made of a large but finite number of relatively fixed terms which are then allowed to occur in a limited number of clearly specified relations, so that it is not the appearance of a word that matters but *the manner of its reappearance*, and that an unspecifiable number of absolutely unique sentences can in this way be composed, as, of course, life is also continuously refreshing itself in a similar fashion.

There are novel sentences which are novel in the same old ways, and there are novel sentences in which the novelty itself is new. In *How to Write* she discusses the reason why sentences are not emotional and paragraphs are, and offers us some sentences which she believes have the emotional balance of the paragraph.

    a. It looks like a garden but he had hurt himself by accident.
    b. A dog which you have never had before has sighed.
    c. A bay and hills hills are surrounded by their having their distance very near.

Compare these with Sterne's:

    d. A cow broke in tomorrow morning to my Uncle Toby's fortifications.

Or with this by Beckett:

    e. Picturesque detail a woman with white hair still young to judge by her thighs leaning against the wall with eyes closed in abandonment and mechanically clasping to her breast a mite who strains away in an effort to turn its head and look behind.

All right, we have answered the bell. Suppose we broke that action into parts: opening the door, coming down the stairs, mewing with annoyance, and so forth—how easily we might combine them in other ways, in new sentences of behavior, new paragraphs of life.

Mewing with annoyance reflects a state more subjective than the others. Mewing with annoyance is an event of lesser size, though it, too, is divisible. All are audible acts, unlike the secretion of saliva. Our sentence must manage them—their motion, weight, size, order, state of being—must be themselves events, must pass through space the way we pass when we skip down the stairs to the door.

Let's begin with a sentence without any special significance, selected the same way you might curiously pick up a piece of paper in the street.

In the middle of the market there's a bin of pumpkins. Dividing this sentence as it seems natural to do, we can commence its conquest:

   a. There's a bin of pumpkins in the middle of the market.

    b. There, in the middle of the market, is a bin of pumpkins.

    c. A bin of pumpkins? There, in the middle of the market.

    d. A bin of . . . pumpkins? There? In the middle of the market?

We can make our arrangements more musical:

    e. In the middle. In the middle of the market. In the middle there's a bin. There's a bin. In the middle of the market there's a bin.

    f. In the middle. In the middle of the market. In the middle of the market there's a bin. A bin. In the middle of the market there's a bin. In. A bin. In. In the market there's a bin. In the middle of the market—pumpkin.

    g. Middle of market. Middle of. Middle of. Middle of market. Middle of bin. In the middle of market a middle of market, in the middle of market there's a middle of bin. In the middle of market, in the middle of bin, there's a middle of pumpkin, there's a middle of in.

    h. Pumpkin. In in in. Pumpkin. In middle. In market. In bin.

Much of this is singsong, of course, but the play has only begun. Besides, this is just a demonstration record. The words themselves can be knocked apart, rhymes introduced, or conceptual possibilities pursued.

 i. Middle of market. Riddle of. Middle of. Riddle of market. Middle of bin. Not thin when in. When hollow in huddle then kindle pumpkin.

 j. Pump. Pump ump. In the middle. P p. Um, there's a bin. Pumpkin.

And so on, and so on.

Such games soon give us an idea of the centers of conceptual energies in any sentence, its flexibility, a feel for the feelings possible for it, all its aural consequences; and to a child who is eagerly looking for a skull to carve some Halloween horror on, our celebration of the sentence will seem perfectly sensible.

The procedure is thoroughly analytical, however. It treats the elements of the sentence as if they were people at a party, and begins a mental play with all their possible relationships. Gertrude Stein's work rarely deals very happily with indivisible wholes.

Sometimes she treats a sentence as if it were a shopping list, and rearranges every item in happier orders, much as we might place knicknacks on a shelf, considering whether the spotted china dog might be seen to better advantage in front of the jade lizard and nearer the window, or beside the tin cup borrowed from a beggar in Beirut.

Sometimes she lets us see and follow every step, but often she neglects to give us the sentences she began with, and we find ourselves puzzled by distant results.

Think next what might happen if we considered the sentence to be composed of various voices: in short, a play. For what else is a play? It simply cites the separate sources of its sentences.

h. 1. Martha.   Pumpkin.
      Mary.   In in in.
      Martha.   Pumpkin.
      Joseph.   In middle.
      John.   In market.
      M. & M.   In bin.

A musician would have no trouble in seeing how a single sentence might be treated as the consequence of a chorus, nor would a modern painter find it hard to imagine the dissolution of his plate, bread, vase, and fish, into plastic elements he then rearranged in a new, more pleasing way.

Gertrude Stein did more with sentences, and understood them better, than any writer ever has. Not all her manipulations are successful, but even at their worst, most boring, most mechanical, they are wonderfully informative. And constantly she thought of them as things in space, as long and wiggling and physical as worms. Here is a description of some of them from "Poetry and Grammar":

. . . my sentences . . . had no longer the balance of sentences because they were not the parts of a paragraph nor were they a paragraph but they had made in so far as they had come to be so long and with a balance of their own that they had they had become something that was a whole thing and in so being they had a balance which was the balance of a space completely not filled but created by something moving as moving is not as moving should be.

She understood reading, for instance. She sometimes read straight on, touching the page as lightly as a fly, but even as her mind moved there would be a halt, a turning, the eyes rising and falling in a wave, and she realized that the page, itself, was artificial, arbitrary with respect to the text, so she included it in the work as well, not as a thing or an action, but as an idea.

j. 1. Page one.   Pump. Pump ump.
      Page two.   In the middle.
      Page three.   P   p.
      Page four.   Um, there's a bin.
      Page five.   Pumpkin.

The understanding was, as she read, not only tormented by the physical makeup of the book, it was often troubled, too, by the content, which it had difficulty in making out. The poem does not repeat itself, but I do. I read the first four lines, and then I reread the first two. Now I am ready to go on, and I jump without a qualm to the second quatrain. Soon, however, I am back at the beginning again. There are interruptions, too. Alice asks me what I would like for dinner. Company comes. Time passes. Other texts may even intervene, many strange words from all directions. Why not, she thought, formalize all this, create something new, not only from the stops and starts and quarrels of normal thought, but from the act of attention itself, and all its snarls and tangles, leaps and stumbles.

She is not always satisfied to merely render the phenomenon. Sometimes she chooses to involve us in it. By removing punctuation, for instance. I am reading her sentence about her sentences, which I quote above, and sliding over words as though through mud:

. . . not filled but created by something moving as moving is not as moving . . .

I must pick myself up. Reread until I get the hang:

. . . not filled, but created by something moving, as moving *is*, not as moving should be.

By the time I understand what she means, *I* have been composed. Thus the repetitions which mimic my own when I read make me repeat even more when I read them written down.

Listen. We converse as we live—by repeating, by combining and recombining a few elements over and over again just as nature does when of elementary particles it builds a world. Gertrude Stein had a wonderful ear and she listened as she listened to Leo—for years—not so she could simply reproduce the talk, that sort of thing was never her intention, but so she could discover the patterns in speech, the *forms* of repetition, and exploit them. At first she saw these shapes as signs of the character of the speaker, but later her aim was to confer upon the words themselves the quality she once traced to the owner of the tongue. That was Cézanne's method—the method of the human mind.

We not only repeat when we see, stand, communicate; we repeat when we think. There's no other way to hold a thought long enough to examine it except to say its words over and over, and the advance of our mind from one notion to another is similarly filled with backs and forths, erasures and crossings-out. The style of *The Geographical History of America* is often a reflection of this mental condition.

Repeating is also naming. Pumpkins have names. They are called pumpkins. But what is the word "pumpkin" called? not Fred, not William, not

Wallaby, but "pumpkin" again. And so we seem to be repeating when we are speaking in the metalanguage, or the overtongue. A division of "pumpkin" into "pump" and "kin" is not a carving of pumpkin. Nor is the finding and baking and eating of one any damage to the word. An actor's gestures name the real ones. Suppose, behind your back, I am making fun of you by imitating your hurried, impatient, heavy-shoed walk, or like an annoying child I echo your talk as you talk; then a round is being formed, a ring made of reality and its shadow, words and their referents, and of course I can dance with my image or with yours very well, mock my own methods, and suddenly discover, in the midst of my game, a meaning that's more than a vegetable's candle-lit face.

The ice cream eaten is desired again, the song sung is resung, and so we often say things over simply because we love to say them over—there is no better reason.

Furthermore, Gertrude Stein knew that masterpieces were, like life itself is everywhere, perfect engines of repetition. Just as leaves multiply along a limb, and limbs alike thicket a trunk, a work of art suffers simultaneous existence in many places, and eventually is read again and again, sometimes loved by the same lips. As Borges has demonstrated so well, when that inspired madman, Pierre Menard, succeeded in writing a chapter or two of *Don Quixote*, word for word the same, his version was both richer and more complex than that of Cervantes. The reverse can also be the case: *Three Lives*, written by any of us now, would not be nearly so remarkable as it was then.

3

How pleasantly a doll can change its age. I do not even have to dress it differently. My eye alters and a few rags bundled about a stick assume a life, a life at any point or period I like, with any sex and any history I choose—pets, presumptions, peeves—mortal or immortal ills. Whether I imagine it's a swatchel or a queen, the stick with its scrappy sleeves remains and is like another Homer to me, focus for my fancies; yet when I open an old album and find my photo, what tells me what the image is, since I've no faithful wad of fabric or enduring spinal tree to fix on? . . . a lingering resemblance? am I that solemn little moon-faced boy in the ribboned hat whose photographic stare is as dumbly inked upon its paper as these words are? am I that weak-eyed, pork-cheeked -creature? . . . possibly; but is it a likeness which leaps out at me, one I feel, or do I have to hunt for it, piously believing that a resemblance must be there, and easily fooled by a substitute, a switch, because a dozen other boys that age may look more like me now than I do then. A sentence with such moods and tenses shows in what strange ways our lifeline's twisted, how precariously it passes from one pole of recognition to another, because, as Hume reported:

For my part, when I enter most intimately into what I call *myself*, I always stumble on some particular perception or other, of heat or cold, light or shade, love or hatred, pain or pleasure. I never can catch *myself* at any time without a perception, and never can observe any thing but the perception. When my perceptions are remov'd for any time, as by sound sleep; so long am I insensible of myself, and may truly be said not to exist.

I may dress Shakespeare, like my dolly, in the costumes of other centuries, interpret him according to the latest scientific myths or social magics, nevertheless there is something—some pale text—some basin, bowl, or bottle I am peeing my opinions in; but as I turn the album pages—black not without a reason—I only dimly remember the bow and arrow in one snapshot, the knickers in another, or the man who was my father holding me wearily in his arms at the entrance to Mammoth Cave. The little boy I was is no longer living with me. Of course, we say that some people never grow up, but the little boy I am at forty is actually the little man I am at forty, no one else.

Rilke's celebrated remark about Rodin sums up
what Gertrude Stein's American trip taught her:

Rodin was solitary before he became famous. And Fame,
when it came, made him if anything still more solitary.
For Fame, after all, is but the sum of all the misunder-
standings which gather about a new name.

Or work of art. It is the same.

When Gertrude Stein wrote that there was little
use in being born a little boy if you were going to grow
up to be a man, she did not intend to deny causality
or the influence of the past. She did mean to say that
when we look at our own life, we are looking at the
history of another; we are like a little dog licking our
own hand, because our sense of ourselves at any time
does not depend upon such data, only our "idea" of
ourselves does, and this "idea," whether it's our own
or that of another, is our identity. Identities depend
upon appearances and papers. Appearances can be
imitated, papers forged.

She also said: I am not I any longer when I see.
Normally, as Schopenhauer first and Bergson later
argued so eloquently, we see like an animal. We see
prey, danger, comfort, security. Our words are tags
which signify our interests: chairs, bears, sunshine,
sex; each is seen in relation to our impulses, instincts,
aims, in the light of our passions, and our thought

about these things is governed entirely by what we consider their utility to be. Words are therefore weapons like the jaws of the crocodile or the claws of the cat. We use them to hold our thought as we hold a bone; we use them to communicate with the pack, dupe our enemies, manipulate our friends; we use them to club the living into food.

When, for instance, we give ourselves to a piece of music—not to drink, daydream, or make. love, but to listen—we literally lose ourselves, and as our consciousness is captured by the music, we are in dreamless sleep, as Hume says, and are no more. We become, in becoming music, that will-less subject of knowing of which Schopenhauer spoke so convincingly.

Human nature is incapable of objectivity. It is viciously anthropocentric, whereas the human mind leaves all personal interest behind. It sees things as entities, not as identities. It is concerned, in the Kantian sense, with things-in-themselves. The human mind knows that men must die that others may live; one epoch go that another may take its place; that ideas, fashions, feelings, pass. The human mind neither forgets nor remembers; it neither sorrows nor longs; it never experiences fear or disappointment. In the table headed Human Nature there is, therefore, time and memory, with all their beginnings, their middles, and their ends; there is habit and identity, storms and hilly country, acting, audience, speaking and adventure, dogs and other animals, politics, propaganda, war, place, practice and its guiding truths, its directing sciences, while in the table of the Human Mind there's contact rather than connection, plains, space, landscape, math and money, not nervousness but excitement, not saying but showing, romance rather than mystery, masterpieces moreover, and above all, Being.

Gertrude Stein was no longer merely explaining herself. She had begun to wonder what it was inside her which had written *Three Lives* rather than the novels of Lew Wallace; what it was that made masterpieces. Besant's books had sold very well and he had been admired. But he had sold to people of principally the same sort and had been read during a finger-snap of time. Masterpieces escaped both country and climate, every condition of daily life; they hurdled history; and it was not because daily life, climate, country, and history were not contents, as if in those sweetly beautiful Angelicos there were no angels. What accounted for it? in reader? writer? work? Her conclusions were not original, although their largely Kantian character is a little surprising for a student of William James and Santayana.

It was not because she was a woman or was butch— her poodles or her Fords, her vests, her friends, her sober life, her so-called curious ways, her Jewishness, none counted. Allegheny, Pennsylvania, had nothing to do with it. Her "scientific" aim in writing *The Making of Americans*, her desire to define "the bottom nature" of everyone who had or could or would be living, was mistaken and had to do with human nature, not the human mind. She had gone on repeating because she thought the world did. The world did, but what the world did, did not matter. *Tender Buttons* was pure composition, like Cézanne, but the *Autobiographies* and *A Long Gay Book*, *Three Lives*, *The Making of Americans*, many of the portraits and the plays, although they were about human nature, were fortunately written by the human mind. And it took another human mind to understand them.

There were people who were no more than their poodles. If their little dog didn't know them, who would they be? Like mirrors they reflected what fell into them, and when the room was empty, when the walls were removed and the stars pinched back in the sky, they were nothing, not even glass.

Naïvely, she thought free people formed themselves in terms of an Emersonian self-reliance; she believed in the frontier, and in the ethic of the pioneer. After all she was one. Naïvely she thought that the average man, here in America, understood the spiritual significance of space, and was less a slave to human nature.

Consequently here the human mind should flourish, the masterpiece emerge, the animal sleep. However, *Finnegans Wake* would demonstrate best the endless roundness she had in mind, and the perfect description of her ideal had long ago appeared, in 1894: Paul Valéry's *Monsieur Teste*.

Just as the order of the numbers in a sum makes no difference, just as there is no special sequence to towns on a map, the mind and the masterpiece may pass back and forth between thoughts as often and as easily as trains between Detroit, Duluth, and Denver, and chapter headings are, in fact, only the names of places. Oral literature had to be sequential (like music before tape), but type made possible a reading which began at the rear, which repeated preferred passages, which skipped. As in an atlas, the order was one of convenience, and everything was flat. A geographical history rolls time out like that. Of course, there are stories still; an evening's entertainment, that's all human nature asks for; but masterpieces have to bear repeating and repeating. There are no surprises, no suspense, no tears, no worries in them. We know what will happen to Ahab. Duncan's dead, and Anna's under her train. I can tell you the page. *The Wings of the Dove* lies spread before us now as openly as Iowa. Literature in the eyes of the human mind is like land seen from a plane. And so is Gertrude Stein when we find her. Macbeth shall murder sleep again, Tom Jones receive a beating, Heathcliff . . . ah, well . . . "Oblige me," she says, "by not beginning." Netherfield Park is let at last. Mr. Gradgrind is still proceeding on the principle that two and two are four, and nothing over. Bloom is carrying a piece of soap about. The next century is approaching like a distant train. John Barth has just written *Chimera*, Beckett has brought out *The Lost Ones*, Nabokov a book called *Transparent Things*. And they are reissuing *The Geographical History of America* almost a hundred years from the author's birthday. Oblige me, she says, "Also by not ending."

William H. Gass

Washington University, St. Louis

THE GEOGRAPHICAL HISTORY
OF AMERICA
OR
THE RELATION OF HUMAN NATURE
TO THE HUMAN MIND

IN the month of February were born Washington Lincoln and I.

These are ordinary ideas. If you please these are ordinary ideas.

Let us talk not about disease but about death. If nobody had to die how would there be room enough for any of us who now live to have lived. We never could have been if all the others had not died. There would have been no room.

Now the relation of human nature to the human mind is this.

Human nature does not know this.

Human nature cannot know this.

What is it that human nature does not know. Human nature does not know that if every one did not die there would be no room for those who live now.

Human nature can not know this.

Now the relation of human nature to the human mind is this.

Human nature cannot know this.

But the human mind can. It can know this.

In the United States there is more space where nobody is than where anybody is.

This is what makes America what it is.

Does it make human nature in America what it is. If not it does make the human mind in America what it is.

But there being so much space in America where nobody is has nothing to do with this that if nobody had ever died that is if everybody had not died there would not be room here for anybody who is alive now.

This is the way human nature can sleep, it can sleep by not knowing this. The human mind can sleep by knowing this. Until it knows this the human mind cannot sleep, and sleep well human nature and the human mind can sleep.

After all would do we like to live to have lived, then if we do then everybody else has had to die and we have to cry because we too one day we too will have to die otherwise the others who will like to live could not come by.

This is what makes religion and propaganda and politics this and with this the human mind and human nature.

And the human mind can know this but human nature cannot know this and so the human mind pretty well does not know this.

A dog can go to sleep standing and not know the reason why.

A man can go to sleep standing and that is the reason why, he can go to sleep standing but he prefers not to.

For this there is no reason why.

Yes and yet this this is what makes everybody say what they do if they do say what they do say.

And everybody does say what they do say.

This makes propaganda and politics and religion.

And some say that we have all these things now.

And have we any of all these things now and have we any reason why why we have these things now but perhaps we have not these things now. A Geographical history is very important when connected with all this.

Nobody knows any more about human nature and the human mind than that.

Individualism that is human nature and the human mind communism that is human nature and the human mind and why do they go on saying so and not.

Because here is the pause they pause and the cause the cause is that they pause and they cannot pause.

Man is man was man will be gregarious and solitary, he will be because it is his nature to he will be because he has a mind to and even once more it is more and more and more as if he wants to.

What has the human mind got to do with talking.

Just that, what you say makes you want to say it again and what you say wants to make you say it another way, say the same thing another or the other thing in some way.

Any way is another way if you say it the same way.

Individualism and communism they are not separate they are the same or else human nature would not be human nature but it is.

Any little dog says so.

He wants to run away and he wants to be there with you.

Oh yes of course but as he has not a human mind he can act so he can do the two things at once but the human mind ah the human mind can not do the two things at once. That is wherein the human mind differs from human nature.

Idem the same.

If you please these are ordinary ideas.

As anybody sits and looks they do not necessarily look to see what they do see.

If they did see they would see that the dog would does run away and stay. Just like this. He feels like that any way.

Now anybody who loves money and anybody who loves loves money anybody who loves loves to have money.

The human mind can say yes and no the human mind can even know that there is yes and no, not every human mind not any human mind but the human mind, the human mind can know that there is yes and no.

Yes that is the way I mean to please.
Think how that sentence goes.
Yes that is the way I mean to, please.
Well anyway.
That is what I mean to be I mean to be the one who can and does have as ordinary ideas as these.

End of Chapter one.

If you stop to think about chapter one you will know that any one has had to die so that there is room for any one to be, that is if every one who had lived had not died where would we be.

In other words if everybody even if there had not been a great many but just only as many as there have been if anybody that is everybody had not died there would not be room here and now for anybody who is here here and now.

Even in America where there is more space where there is nobody than where there is. Never to forget that.

These are ordinary ideas.

Chapter II

Extraordinary ideas.

Extraordinary ideas are just as ordinary as ordinary ideas because if you please everybody has to have or have had extraordinary ideas.

Do extraordinary ideas interfere with propaganda and communism and individualism and what are any and all ideas.

To know what ideas are you have to think of geographical history and the relation of the human mind to human nature.

What do they say.

What is the use of being a little boy if you are growing up to be a man.

What is the use of Franklin Roosevelt being like the third Napoleon.

What is the use.

What is the use of being a little boy if you are to grow up to be a man.

Chapter III

What is the use of being a little boy if you are going to grow up to be a man.

Neither human nature or the human mind thinks so. They do not think that there is no use in being a little boy if you are going to grow up to be a man.

And yet everybody does so unless it is a little girl going to grow up to be a woman.

But what is the use.

Use is here used in the sense of purpose.

Does it interfere with propaganda to really know this

thing, what is the use of being a little boy if you are going to grow up to be a man.

Chapter one

What do they say.

They say that Washington and Lincoln and I were born in that month the month of February and that this nobody can deny.

February is a short month but although February is a short month we Washington Lincoln and I were born in that month in that short month.

Not even now again can any one this deny, not they nor not I.

Chapter II

The human mind fails to be a human mind when it thinks because it cannot think that what is the use of being a little boy if you are going to grow up to be a man.

Now let the human mind think what it is to be a little boy and when the human mind has thought what it is to be a little boy the human mind will know that there is no use in being a little boy if you are going to grow up to be a man.

Human nature can not know that there is no use in being a little boy if he is to grow up to be a man.

There is then a connection between human nature and the human mind insofar as human nature cannot know that there is no use in being a little boy if he is to grow up to be a man and the human mind can well yes it can if it can it can know that there is no use in being a little boy if he is to grow up to be a man.

And then as it is to have these human nature and the human mind and the little boy and he has to grow up to be a man and is there any use in all of these then there is a geographical history of all these, you do feel that as it is where it is.

I can just see the way the land lies as all of these are there. And so can you. And so can you.

There is no question not any question as to which land lies over or under the seas. Salt lake country is over and under the seas only there is no sea. So much better that there is no sea because then the land can be seen and can see.

Chapter III which is the same as chapter XV

Do you see that there is the land which nobody can see because there is the sea, and yet there is the land in America there is the land salt lake land where there is no sea.

Chapter III

How can you tell if a country is young old or young young or old.

Is it because all the animals that have lived on it are dead in it.

Chapter IV

As long as nothing or very little that you write is published it is all sacred but after it is a great deal of it published is it everything that you write is it as sacred. That has to do with whether the animals dead in it make a country as old as if no animals were dead in it.

Has this to do with human nature or the human mind.

And does any one need to wonder why.

So in chapter three we consider these things the age of the world, the sacredness of writing and human nature and the human mind.

and
Geographical History.
Chapter III

What is the relation of human nature to the age of any country.

One cannot say it too often and it need not bring tears to your eyes what is the use of being a little boy if you are going to grow up to be a man what is the use.

An age of a country is not the same thing because after all it may be it even might be that human nature has nothing to do with it. But the human mind must have something to do with it although when to the human mind that country is old and when to the human mind that country is young that country need not necessarily be either young or old. Has the human mind really has the human mind anything to do with age or is that only human nature, human nature has undoubtedly to do with age but has the human mind, neither more nor less but has the human mind. Let me now in Chapter IV tell any story of Geography and what it looks like and the human mind.

Chapter IV

Geography does not look like it does in relation to the human mind.

Not more or less but to begin with what man is man was man will be.

When children play tag they tag each other that is they touch each other to start, well dogs do that, they touch each other to start just as children do. A big dog touches a little dog to start him to play a white dog touches a black dog to start him to play a black dog will touch any dog to start him to play. When children do so it is called playing tag.

Any child does that.

And has the human mind anything to do with kidnapping perhaps yes perhaps no. Kidnapping means that they take anything away. But the human mind can never take anything away.

Dogs do so they mean and they do not mean to do so.

But dogs cannot say I mean I mean. They can though they can say I mean I mean and they do, they also can say I forgot and they do they do both forget and they do say so and there is a reason why.

Anybody with a human mind can say I mean and they can say I forgot and mean that. Fighting is not an action of the human mind neither is remembering if it had to do with the human mind then the human mind would concern itself with age but it does not, therefore any nature can mean or not mean what they do they can forget or remember what they do but the human mind no the human mind has nothing to do with age.

As I say so tears come into my eyes.

Why does the human mind not concern itself with age.

Because the human mind knows what it knows and knowing what it knows it has nothing to do with seeing what it remembers, remember how the country looked as we passed over it, it made designs big designs like human nature draws them because it knows them without ever having seen them from above.

Why in an aeroplane is one not afraid of being high.

Because human nature has nothing to do with it.

Nothing.

I repeat yes and no nothing.

When you climb on the land high human nature

knows because by remembering it has been a dangerous thing to go higher and higher on the land which is where human nature was but now in an aeroplane human nature is nothing remembering is nothing no matter how many have been killed from up there it is not anything that is a memory, because if you are killed you do not remember no you do not, it is only on land where it is dangerous but where you were not killed that you remember.

And so the human mind is like not being in danger but being killed, there is no remembering, no there is no remembering and no forgetting because you have to remember to forget no there is none in any human mind.

This brings us back to tag and kite flying and kidnapping and how they are related to the human mind.

Chapter V

The human mind when it is altogether the human mind what a pleasure to me. No this does not bring tears to anybody's eyes not even to mine and I might I might cry easily oh so very easily.

Kidnapping kite flying and tag and labor unions and the Republican party and the human mind and what eight or as many places look like when it is just as high as it is when you pass over.

Looking down is the same as passing over.

Snow is always astonishing when it is looked at.

But not more astonishing when the trees the bare trees make shadows on it.

Dogs do behave as they please that is as they naturally please until they are told not to.

Anything like that is annoying and annoying has something to do with the human mind. It means it is attached and waits not to go away but to stay. In this way annoying or annoyance is a symptom of there being a human mind.

Yes a human mind.

And what is it.

Is it that all the same.

Chapter III

Beginning with tears.

Annoyance makes nobody cry.

But something does oh yes something does but should it.

Who has to know what word follows another.

I do. Although it is a mistake.

The human mind is not unlike that.

I do. Although it is perfectly a mistake.

If perfection is good more perfection is better is not said but might be said of the human mind.

Chapter IV

But any way any man that is women and children can talk all day or a piece of any day, dogs do too not in the same way not quite in the same way and that does make some difference between human beings and dogs.

I wish I could say that talking had to do with the human mind I wish I could say so and not cry I wish I could.

Chapter V

Does he or she does she or he know what the human mind is.

And so all the old chapters end tears end but all this has nothing to do with the human mind the use of the human mind and tears.

It has been said said by very many said by Jules Verne he weeps that shows he is a man. But a dog can have tears in his eyes yes he can have tears in his eyes when he has been disillusioned.

A dog when he begged always got what he asked for.

One day he begged a little dog to give him what he wanted. The little dog did not give him what he wanted. The dog had tears in his eyes and so to cry does not make the human mind oh no to cry does not make the human mind it makes a piece of nature but it does not make the human mind.

The human mind has nothing to do with sorrow and with disappointment and with tears.

You can say to a dog look and long and he does, he even does without your saying so but and that is true human nature can look and long but not the human mind no not the human mind.

Oh dear does she does he does he does she know what the human mind is and if he does and if she does and if she does and if he does what is the human mind.

The human mind knows neither memory nor tears it can forget, but what can it forget, it can forget nothing but not be remembering indeed not by remembering and so he and she and she and he do know what the human mind is.

A dog does not know what the human mind is.

He only knows grief and disturbance and tears he only knows that if he has lost confidence he has lost confidence and he was born with that confidence lost.

The relation of human nature to the human mind makes everybody indifferent to remembering and forgetting to age and living to knowing that every one can die so that there may be room for all who are here now and so many people expect to prepare otherwise but they they do not know what the human mind is.

If there was no geography no geographical history would there be any human mind not as it is but would there would there be any human mind.

Anybody that can help this to go farther can go on with what the human mind is and so as indifferently as that we begin with Chapter one.

Chapter I

The human mind is.

The human mind has no relation to human nature at all. The question has been asked is it the relation of human nature to the human mind or is it the relation of the human mind to human nature. The answer is there is no relation between the human mind and human nature there is a relation between human nature and the human mind.

Chapter one

What is it.

Chapter III

Does or does not a dog know that there is a human mind, no he does not know that there is a human mind he knows that there is human nature but not that there is a human mind.

Is or is not a dog born with his confidence gone. This is not an interesting question.

Chapter III

What is the relation of communism individualism propaganda to human nature what is the relation of it to the human mind or is there none. There is a human mind oh yes there is one. Is there any relation to it in communism individualism or propaganda or has all that only to do with human nature, has it has it, remember about tears and age and memory and swallows flying and birds which always sing the same thing to any one but not to themselves, they the birds have tears but no memory.

How many animals birds and wild flowers are there in the United States and is it splendid of it to have any.

There are some places in the United States where they almost do not have any.

The United States is interesting because in it there are some in it that have no human nature at all just as in some places in it there are almost not any animals or flowers at all and this what has this to do with the relation of human nature to the human mind.

Anybody can have tears in their eyes when they hear dogs bark. Because which of it is it.

Chapter IV

Why Europe is too small to wage war.

Why is Europe too small to wage war because war has to be waged on too large a scale to be contained in a small country therefore as they think about war they know that they can only think and not do. They are like our dogs who make believe do things to each other but they know that they can be seen and if you can be seen then you cannot do anything to one another.

Therefore Europe is too small to wage war since anybody now can see it all and if anybody really anybody can see it all then they cannot wage war. They can have a great many troubles but they cannot wage war. Not wage war.

Also the geographical history of America.

Chapter V

Madame Reverdy was the wife of a hotel keeper. I say was because she is dead not awfully dead but still dead.

One of the things that makes a big country different from a little country makes the Geographical history of America different from the geographical history of Europe is that when anybody is dead they are dead.

So Madame Reverdy was the wife of a hotel keeper. In many hotels in small countries they never go out of the hotel. She never did and neither did he. He is not dead, not because he could live longer but because he is not dead.

She had four children that is they did three boys and a girl and the girl had a curl but she got very stout. She still is but not as stout as she was.

The three boys were very good looking when they were younger.

Now it is just the same as the older is married and the younger is a one lunger and the third is a cook. But all this had not happened when the mother was no longer their mother as she had become dead that is she had killed herself just as much to be dead as not. No one asked her to live longer but if she did it she did it not to live longer but to be a hotel keeper longer.

She had been awfully ready to be a hotel keeper but she had been not awfully ready not to live longer. She is dead as much dead as if she had not lived longer.

No one can care to know what happens to any one although everybody listens to any one who tells about what happened to any one.

I feel that it is a failure not to live longer.

So they say.

And so Europe can stay but it cannot wage war any longer.

This is what all the world is that it cannot wage war any longer and so it might just as well stop. Human nature is not interesting any longer and so it might just as well stop being human nature any longer.

Chapter VI

The portrait of Thornton Wilder.

In china china is not china it is an earthen ware. In China there is no need of China because in China china is china.

All who liked china like china and have china.

China in America is not an earthen ware.

All who like china in America like china in America and all who like china in America do not like to have china in china be an earthen ware. Therefore it is not.

Remember therefore it is not but better not remember.

It is better not to remember because there is no such thing no such thing as remember. Therefore there is not.

All allow no one allow, no one to allow no one to remember.

It is left to be right not to remember because not to remember is as much left as not left to remember.

It is no doubt a resistance to yield to all. Not to yield at all.

Oh no remember there is a great difference between to yield at all but not to yield to all.

Do not remember because it is not to remember that makes it be theirs as well as the.

A portrait celebrated as the portrait of Thornton Wilder.

I wish I knew a history was a history.

And tears.

I wish I knew a history as a history which is not which is not there are no fears.

He has no fears.

At most he has no tears.

For them very likely he is made of them.

It is too bad that fears rhymes with tears.

Very likely for them.

But which I beseech you to say.

Chapter VII

I cannot be accused too often of liking to hear and see everything and yet everything which is heard and which is seen has nothing no nothing no no nothing to do with the human mind. No nothing.

And yet the human mind there is the human mind.

Human nature now is not at all interesting.

Chapter II

Did you hear your husband heave a heavy sigh.

Nobody knows how happy it is to have anything sound like that.

This chapter is to be all about when words how words do words look like that.

Like it did when I looked at it, there there where I saw it.

Beneath me when I was above it.

If there was only human nature there would be words but they would not be like that.

Chapter III

There is no real reality to a really imagined life any more.

Nothing I like more than when a dog barks in his sleep.

That is a reality that can be known not by listening but by the dog who is asleep and feels like barking, he barks as if he barks and it is a bark it really is a bark although he is only dreaming. How much does he know that he is barking.

Human nature moves around and does the human mind move around.

What is the difference between remembering what has been happening and remember what has been as dreaming. None. Therefore there is no relation between human nature and the human mind.

When they say do not read or know this because you do not understand it what does it mean.

To understand a thing means to be in contact with that thing and the human mind can be in contact with anything.

Human nature can be connected with anything but it can not be in contact with anything.

Any minute then is anything if there is a human mind.

Any minute is not anything if there is human nature.

But any minute is anything so then there is a human mind.

Think of how very often there is not, there is not a human mind and so any minute is not anything.

Any one can see that human nature can not make any minute be anything.

They ask me is there any progressing and I answer and now human nature is not interesting why of course not it is not interesting. It is there to be sure it is there but just now it is not interesting.

Chapter I

One and one makes two but not in minutes. No never again in minutes.

That is what is the human mind. There is nothing in it about minutes. Progressing of course there is no progressing no there is the human mind not interesting but being there yes just as well as not.

Chapter II

If some one says and how is Rachel and you say very well I thank you that means that Rachel does belong to you.

How is America. Very well I thank you. This is the

reply. If you say I thank you that means that in a way it belongs to you. Very well I thank you.

Human nature is what any human being will do. And the human mind. Tears come into my eyes when I say the human mind. Tears do not come into my eyes they are the feeling of tears my eyes are the feeling of tears. And not because I say the human mind. But because there is the human mind. Oh yes there is a human mind. Not entirely at a glance not at all at a glance. When she says look at the roses is that human nature or the human mind.

She will tell me, yes she will tell me if when she says look at the roses whether that is human nature or the human mind.

Human nature is what any human being will do.

That is a very satisfactory thing to say.

And the human mind is the way they tell what any human being has or does or may or can do.

Not at all not at all not at all.

That has nothing to do with the human mind. That is the same thing as saying that human speech is the same thing as the human mind and it is not.

Whether or whether not the human mind could exist if there had been no human speech this I do not know but this I do know that the human mind is not the same thing as human speech. Has one anything to do with the other is writing a different thing, oh yes and this is so exciting so satisfying so tender that it makes every-thing everything writing has nothing to do with the hu-man speech with human nature and therefore and therefore it has something to do with the human mind.

Take an example a dog can tag another dog to start him playing and he remembers this and does it again not because it is the way he remembers it but because it is the way he does.

Now a little girl or boy tags too to start the other one but he says so he says I tagged you and he says I will tag you and he says did you tag him and he says I can tag you if I want to.

That might be the human mind but it is not.

Any little child has to be taught to play tag because although any dog does play tag this way and so any child can play tag this way any child can be taught to be play tag this way.

This has nothing to do with human nature this has to do with the human mind.

So then human nature can talk but so can any dog.

But the human mind can write and so cannot any dog and so human writing is not human nature it is the human mind.

What it looks like when it sees when it is seen, that may make human nature what it is but not the human mind although tears can almost come to its eyes, oh not the human mind, no not the human mind.

When any one looks and sees how what it sees looks like it cannot not know whether it is human nature or the human mind but it can know it will know and therefore as it looks at it all it can know that human nature is not the human mind. Once as a piece. Or even twice or more as a piece.

A piece is only a little way and it must finish even if the world is round and the land on it is flat as it is like a carpet as it is but the human mind can not remember that. The human mind can not remember no cannot remember, yes that is that.

When anything looks like it is and it is land and anybody writing or painting says it is that no one needs to remember that.

Chapter IX

How looking at it does not make it different from what it looks like.

That is why they make it like that not because they look at it but because it is like that. Yes the human mind.

Chapter X

A description of how the land the American land the land in America looks and is flat is and looks flat.

Chapter I

Some dogs eyes in the night give out a red ruby light and some dog's eyes at night are green.

Has this anything to do with the human mind. It might.

It can have nothing to do with human nature that can easily be seen. Seen is here used in the sense of known.

All these things have something to do with excitement and has excitement anything to do with the human mind.

Any dog can get excited he can know that he can get excited and he can know that he intends to get excited and he can gradually get forced to get excited although he does not care about it. Human nature is like that and the human mind. Here we commence to come to one of the complete problems concerning the human mind. I must ask every one with or without tears in my eyes has excitement anything to do with the human mind.

Has it to do with geography.

It has undoubtedly to do with politics and propaganda and government and being here and there and society has it anything to do with writing. Has it in short has it now there are no tears in my eyes has it to do with the human mind.

Chapter II

What has excitement got to do with geography and how does the land the American land look from above from below and from custom and from habit.

Are there any customs and habits in America there is geography and what what is the human mind. The human mind is there because they write and they do not forget or remember and they do not go away and come back again. That is what the human mind does not human nature but the human mind. Listen to the human mind.

I will tell a story about the human mind what is the story.

It is the story of Bennett.

Bennett has an uncle who is as young as he is that is to say he is about the same age and age has nothing to do with the human mind.

When a great many hear you that is an audience and if a great many hear you what difference does it make.

Bennett and his uncle do not know anything about that.

And why not. Because that has nothing to do with the human mind.

Bennett's uncle has nothing to do with the human mind because he listens to the human mind and if you listen to the human mind is there a human mind to which you listen.

Bennett's uncle has nothing to do with human nature because human nature well if you have tears for human nature and gradually human nature has no tears how can you have human nature.

And this and this brings us to this that human nature has now no tears and this this is all because of the history of geography, geography now having come to be what it is the land lying as it does and any one looking at it seeing it as it is there are no more tears in human nature.

And so where where is Bennett's uncle, he is not with the human mind because he listens to the human mind and he is not with human nature because there are no tears in human nature. Where is Bennett. Bennett is not there, because Bennett does not listen to the human mind and because he has no tears with human nature and so Bennett is what he is. And what is that and how many are that.

It has been said, that if everybody had gone on living there would not be any room here now where we all are for those of us who are here now this includes Bennett and Bennett's uncle. And this would make his uncle cry if every one were to die but not Bennett Bennett would not cry because Bennett as Bennett knows that he is human nature and human nature does not cry not now not unless human nature is tired human nature can be tired but is human nature tired now, no not now.

Is it exciting not to cry. Yes and no and Bennett knows that this is so.

Chapter III

There are no chapters in the life of Bennett but there are chapters in the life of the Uncle of Bennett because he knows and as he knows he knows that some time is a time that he can look forward and remember and if you can then that is not the human mind. The human mind cannot does not look forward and remember and so really and truly Bennett's uncle cannot listen to the human mind. And so he is a communist. A communist and individualist a propagandist a politician cannot listen to the human mind, a business man can and anybody who can sit and write can he can listen to the human mind. Can Bennett, well I do not know whether Bennett can.

What you cannot eat you can.

Yes Bennett.

Chapter IV

The world as we see it looks like this.

They used to think that the world was there as we see it but this is not so the world is there as it is human nature is there as it is and the human mind. The human mind knows this, that everything is there as it is.

Only the human mind knows this and that is the reason that it is not what anybody says but what anybody writes that has to do what it has to do with the human mind.

That is what makes the comic strip, Mr. and Mrs. the success it is, it is that the human mind knows that it is what it is. It even knows that human nature is what it is therefore it need not remember or forget no the human mind does not remember because how can you remember when anything is what it is.

Or how can you forget when anything is what it is.

Bless a wife who has made this clear.

Chapter V

And so a great many birds hop and sing.
Anything is what it is.

Chapter VI

There are birds in America but I have not noticed them not as much as I have noticed them here.

There are a great many birds in America but I did not notice them.

I do notice them here. You notice birds if you sit with them. That is natural as birds are always twittering singing and flying. They come in and go out again so naturally as with the dogs you notice them if you are sitting.

I noticed some animals over there, it is natural to notice them as if they were wild ones living naturally where
they used to be wild ones.

By their used to be wild ones it is meant that no one
was interested then in their being there except as they
were there that is when they were wild ones as if they
were wild ones. Now they see to it that they are still wild
but continue to be there. That is what makes it be
America over there that no one knows the difference
between human nature and the wild animals there because there is more not being wild but being ones there
there is more now there that they live as easily as anything since no one intends any things should happen to
any one of them. In other words there in America wild
ones are as if they were there with nothing to happen to
them as if they lived there which they do so that nobody
thinks they die there which they do.

That is what peace is but always there is some one
who has not felt that this could be done that any wild
animal living where it is living could naturally go on
being living until it became dead. Dead is not uninteresting and yet it is not any more uninteresting than that
to any animal or human nature.

So that is peace.

Suddenly it comes to be that anybody can be peace-
fully not knowing any other thing.

Has that anything to do with the land as it is and the human mind.

Just as likely as not there are no tears.

She says she wanted that she should be the only ideal one, but she is, what else is she but that, she is, and so the human mind rests with what is.

Yes which it is, that.

That is what they call it. That.

Chapter VII

Now I wish to say just what human nature is and what its relation is to the human mind.

I know so well the relation of a simple center and a continuous design to the land as one looks down on it, a wandering line as one looks down on it, a quarter section as one looks down on it, the shadows of each tree on the snow and the woods on each side and the land higher up between it and I know so well how in spite of the fact that the human mind has not looked at it the human mind has it to know that it is there like that, notwithstanding that the human mind has liked what it has which has not been like that.

Has the human mind anything to do with what it sees. Yes I think so. With what it likes. No I do not think so. With what it has. No I do not think so, with communism individualism propaganda politics and

77

women no and yes I think so, I think it is not so. With the world as it has said it was. No I do not think so. Then what is the human mind. Has the human mind anything to do with question and answer. Perhaps no I do not think so.

Chapter IV

They say I am not right when I say that what you say is not the same as what you write but anybody try to write and they will say that this is so.

When you write well when you write anybody try to write and they will say that I am right.

What you say has nothing to do with what you write.

Does it rain in America oh yes and there is snow. High up and low down there is snow, snow snow really beautiful snow.

What is the difference between anything and anything.

Ah yes, well that is something to know.

What is the difference between as snow and as snow.

They say that when I say it is not what they say but what they write that has to do with the human mind they say when I say this that I am not right but I am right because I write this and I do not say this. When I say it it is not so but when I write it it is so. Anybody can know that this is so.

And so we come to what is really what we write what we write is really a crime story.

Why the writing of to-day has to do with the way any land can lay when it is there particularly flat land. That is what makes land connected with the human mind only flat land a great deal of flat land is connected with the human mind and so America is connected with the human mind, I can say I say so but what I do is to write it so. Think not the way the land looks but the way it lies that is now connected with the human mind.

And so and so and there is no real use for tears.

Only when her son has fallen off a cart and when the small bones of his ankle are broken in the midst of the harvest and he cannot work for two months. Then it is nervousness that makes water come into her eyes.

Chapter II

The use of the human mind and its connection with what is being written.

Think of what anybody does they read what is or has been written. They do not read what is or has been said. Even on the radio it is written it is not said no no not said.

Chapter III

You will find that all this is true when I get through.

Chapter I

All the witnesses of the autobiography are not filled with tears. If they are they are tears of anger not tears of sorrow and nervousness and excitement but really and truly it is necessary to cry when you read anything, crying gives pleasure to reading, but it has nothing to do with the human mind, it has nothing to do with writing.

But not in the home. Tears do not give pleasure in the home. They give pleasure in reading.

Does this show that reading has something to do with the human mind. It has been said that no one but human beings weep and therefore tears show that there is a human mind. Not in the home I repeat not in the home but in reading yes in reading.

And so listen, nervousness makes tears and reading. Sorrow is another thing, sorrow can connect with reading. And so so many people read just as so many people sorrow they do not borrow sorrow nor reading, and what is its connection with the human mind.

It makes me uneasy when I think that here there is a question of the relation of human nature to the human mind and yet I am so sure that there is none no connection between human nature and the human mind no relation between human nature and the human mind.

Chapter II

The Witnesses of my autobiography. Think what an

admirable title that would make for an autobiography think only think how many different titles have been invented for autobiographies, just think only think and it is astonishing always astonishing how many people can think of a new title for an autobiography. And yet autobiographies have nothing to do with the human mind, and they really have nothing to do with tears and reading. When they said reading made easy reading without tears and some one sent me such a beautiful copy of that, does that mean that tears have to do with the human mind as has been so often said.

And now there are no tears in reading. A movie star said, no matter how much or how many cry on the screen the audience remains dry eyed. Has that something to do with the fact that now there is no connection no relation between reading and the human mind.

Does it come down to that.

Has the human mind forgotten to come down to that.

I have been told that I have always been nervous and unoccupied, that I have never cared to fill my time with the things that fill it and that as a result I am not likely to remember or forget and therefore have I a human mind. Is it because of this that I have a human mind. Is it because of this that any one that has a human mind does that, does nothing to fill it.

Is that what makes it that.

And therefore there are no witnesses to the autobiography of any one that has a human mind.

Is this all that makes it that.

There is no reason why chapters should succeed each other since nothing succeeds another, not now any more. In the old novels yes but not now any more and so the human mind not succeeding one thing by another supposing everybody doing nothing should continue living. How about it.

Has that anything to do with the human mind.

No not when it is just like that.

The minute it means anything it has nothing to do with the human mind, with human nature yes, but not with the way the earth is and looks and not with the human mind. No nothing to do with the human mind.

Every body knows just now how nothing succeeds anything. And so just now yes just now the human mind is the human mind.

Chapter III

Venus is so big that it can have a ring around it like the moon. Jo Alsop.

Chapter IV

I wish to show Jo Alsop why the human mind is not what he recognises when he says some minds say what they say. Any word can say something but really that has nothing to do with the human mind. Let me make this clear to Jo Alsop. He is not a witness to an autobiography. Therefore he should be again told what is the human mind. He has not to be told what is human nature because he is not interested in human nature but he has to be told what is the human mind because although he is interested in the human mind he does not know that the human mind is not related to human nature.

Listen Jo Alsop while I make this clear.

Chapter V

Why is it not necessary to have chapters and if in spite of it not being necessary one does have them why do they not have to follow one another.

Nothing is known of the word necessary but Jo Alsop knows something of the word necessary oh yes he does, he says not but oh yes he does and is it because he does know something about the word necessary he does not know anything about the human mind. No one who knows the word necessary can say that he does or does not like it but Jo Alsop can. He can and he does.

Let us not weep for Jo Alsop or have tears in our eyes or in his.

And yet.

Once more the word necessary is not displaced. The human mind cannot be displaced. In that respect it is not the same as the word necessary.

Rest carefully to-night.

Chapter IV

Carefully is such a sweet word.

Chapter V

I do not know where I am going but I am on my way and then suddenly well not perhaps suddenly but perhaps yes I do know where I am going and I do not like it like that.

Because of this there is no such thing as one and one.

That has a great deal to do with the relation of human nature to the human mind it also has a great deal to do with the geographical history of America.

When suddenly you know that the geographical history of America has something to do with everything it may be like loving any man or any woman or even a little or a big dog. Yes it may, that is to say it does.

And why.

Why has nothing to do with that.

Some people like a big country and some people like a little one but it all depends it depends whether you can wander around a big one or a little one. Wandering around a country has something to do with the geographical history of that country and the way one piece of it is not separated from any other one. Can one say too often just as loving or tears in one's eyes that the straight lines on the map of the United States of America make wandering a mission and an everything and can it only be a big country that can be like that or even a little one. Anyway it has a great deal to do with the relation between human nature and the human mind and not remembering and not forgetting and not as much as much having tears in one's eyes. No no tears in one's eyes, whatever any one else can say. In wandering around a big country some people who live in a big country do not wander. What has wandering got to do with the human mind or religion. But really wandering has something to do with the human mind. A big or a little country. Wandering in a big or a little country.

The relation of nervousness to excitement and the death and the death of René Crevel. René Crevel was not nervous he really was not excited and that is because he was in a country where no one wanders.

Chapter V

Any time after a war any one is nervous. They think they are excited but they are nervous.

You can see how that brings wandering and the human mind nearer nearer to what, nearer to nearer. But nervous has nothing to do with the human mind. Whether excitement has we do not yet know but we think so.

Chapter VI

Any one any time after a war is nervous.

They are not excited they are nervous and that has nothing to do either with human nature nor with the human mind.

Human nature has nothing to do with being nervous. When a dog is nervous it has nothing to do with the human mind.

And so rightly so being nervous has nothing to do with the relation of human nature to the human mind.

But has it to do with the human mind.

Chapter VII

How slowly nervousness is everything, and that is not true of excitement, which is not true of anything.

Has excitement anything to do with the human mind.

No hesitating.

Has excitement anything to do with the human mind. When you come as near as that to anything, it has nothing to do with nervousness.

Nervousness has nothing to do with anything but it always is there after a big war.

Please play and pay all respect to the dead, but not in America not where a country is so big that it is divided one part from the other by ruled lines and it has to be flat, it has to be flat, or there is no hope of it not paying respect to the dead.

René Crevel would have liked to have gone to America he always hoped for that.

But now he is dead.

He killed himself.

There is respect for the dead but not over there because so much of the land is flat.

I like it like that.

Chapter II

I could have begun with Chapter I but anybody even I have had enough of that.

Chapter II

But which are they when once a day they do not eat and they do not go away.

Mushrooms are very good to eat.

But we never gave any of them to René Crevel.

What is the relation of the human mind to a real person who has really lived or one that you mix up with whether he has really never been here or not.

We do not change when René Crevel has not been not ever been here yet.

Nobody ever heard of him but what has that to do with whether you will be excited about him.

Nothing at all nothing at all nothing at all.

And if he was all made up.

Something as well would have to do with human nature.

And the human mind.

I wonder.

Chapter III

I like the human mind.

Chapter IV

Human nature.

Human nature does not excite me but it does make me nervous.

Therefore human nature is like a great war, it makes you nervous.

It is not nervous but it makes you nervous.

And as it makes you nervous it has nothing to do with excitement or with the human mind.

I almost like all who tell me so.

And everybody tells me so tells me that human nature has nothing to do with excitement or the human mind because human nature makes you nervous.

And politics and geography and government and propaganda, well and what of it what of politics and geography and government and money and propaganda, do they make you nervous. Do they.

PART II

Chapter I

There is always a relation between one thing and any other thing such as human nature and the human mind, between painting and what you paint between a black and a white dog although they are not related to each other.

Being a relation is one thing.

Just to-day I said is she a mother or a daughter.

Well anyway it might be thought that anyway she would have had to have been a daughter.

But not at all she might have been a granddaughter.

Being a relation is not a necessary thing.

Jo Alsop is he a relation.

Perhaps not.

René Crevel was.

Thornton Wilder is.

Sometimes some one is as if he were an only son.

But is he a son at all.

May be he never has been.

Chapter II

It is very painful if it is true that not every nightingale can sing.

I could not say this thing because I have never listened to any nightingale who could not sing.

I have listened when they began.

Is beginning singing.

For them they know that in America there are no nightingales although there are mocking birds.

And what have the mocking birds done.

They have spread.

They used to be only in the Eastern south, and now they go farther and farther North and they have gone West to Los Angeles and further and further north perhaps they will be all over, the national bird of the United States.

Some one who was born in California had never even heard one before.

All these things must be remembered in the relation of human nature to the human mind and the geographical history of America.

Chapter II

I should have hated the weather had it not been a pleasure, not to hate the weather but to like cold weather. Weather has nothing to do with the human mind neither cold nor hot nor temperate nor violent weather. It has one may almost say nothing to do with human nature.

What is human nature.

Human nature resembles the nature that any human beings have. It is not necessarily it but it resembles it.

How can anything be dull even death if nothing resembles it. Whether they write or whether they do not they could not write if anything did or did not resemble any other thing. This is very important and no one can disturb anybody or anything.

Resemble and disturb.

Dogs play whether they want to or not with each other.

And now.

What is the resemblance between human nature and the human mind.

The human mind has no resemblances if it had it could not write that is to say write right.

There that is better than not said.

Chapter III

It is very likely that something always takes a long time.

A play.

I say two dogs, but say a dog and a dog.

The human mind. The human mind does play. Of course the human mind does play.

Human nature. No human nature does not play, it might desire something but it does not play.

A dog plays because he plays again.

The human mind plays because it plays.

Human nature does not play because it does not play again.

And so to make nervousness and not excitement into a play.

And then to make excitement and not nervousness into a play.

And then to make a play with just the human mind.

Let us try.

A Play.

Make. There is no place to wait.

Wilder. Made is not past make.

Call it all to order because perhaps here there has not been it all kept entirely in the human mind.

And so to begin again.

Make. No instance of make.

Wilder. Do not change wild to wilder.

Now make a play with human nature and not anything of the human mind.

Pivoines smell like magnolias.

Dogs smell like dogs.

Men smell like men.

And gardens smell differently at different seasons of the year.

This is a mistake this is not human nature it comes more nearly having to do with the human mind.

Try a play again.

Even those who are just ordinary know what the human mind is. But not when they are drunk. Nobody knows what the human mind is when they are drunk.

Every little play helps.

Another play.

There is any difference between resting and waiting.

Be careful of analysis and analogy.

A play.

There is no in between in a play.

A play could just as well only mean two.

Then it could do.

It could really have to do

With the human mind.

This is reading without tears but is there writing without tears.

Yes there is when you have been told not to cry.

Chapter IV

Everybody who has a grandfather has had a great grandfather and that great grandfather has had a father. This actually is true of a grandmother who was a granddaughter and her grandfather had a father.

He had brothers and they lived on where he had come from. They always wrote to one another. At anytime anybody who knows how to write can write to one another.

But what do they write about.

They tell about the weather and sometimes what they have sold never what they have given to one another because and never forget that, they always have they always did they always can sell anything that is something to one another.

You may say I think you may say that no one can really give anything to anybody but anybody can sell something to somebody.

This is what makes the human mind and not human nature although a great many one might say anybody can say something about this not being so. But it is so.

And the human mind can live does live by anybody being able to sell something to somebody. That is what money is not give but sell.

Believe it or not that is what money is and what the human mind is. The human nature perhaps not but of what interest is human nature. Any dog that does what it does does what human nature does and if not but if not why not and if why not what interest is that to the human mind. None at all. That is what the human mind is that human nature is not of any interest to it, it is not in any relation to it. That is why sex and jealousy is not the human mind it is human nature and therefore those any one writing letters does not write about that, they write about the weather and money and the family in its relation to money and the weather. Very likely not but most certainly so.

The grandfather of the grandmother went to America and there he was and now in reading all the letters he wrote to his brothers and they wrote to him he never mentioned anything but the weather and money and they always wrote about the weather and money and the family in their relation to so and so that is to weather and money and each other whether they had to do with each other and money and weather.

This is what they really do.

The newspapers tell about events but what have events to do with anything nothing nothing I tell you nothing events have nothing to do with anything nothing, the family of the grandfather and the grandmother was not interested in events because they did not know them and so they told about the weather and money and now everybody knows about the events but really nobody tells them they are still only interested in the weather and money.

Sure that is the way it is.

And why not. Of course there is not a why not.

Now that is one thing.

The other thing is that all the years and now it makes a good many years since the first real author wrote what he had to say, China or Jews or Greeks or anybody else of who is whose, well what of it why this of it that reading it is alright now, now and then what is it, what they wrote they wrote and anybody can read anything anybody wrote.

Do you see that that means that events have nothing to do with the human mind nor has human nature anything to do with the human mind.

I wish it was as clear to anybody as it is to me even if it is not clear to me.

No she is not jealous she is clear about the necessity of being here.

Oh yes oh yes.

Feel quietly about feathers and goats.

If you say so that has to do with the human mind but not with human nature.

How easily it is not pleasurable to have to know about human nature.

But about the human mind the human mind is pleasurable it is only pleasurable and therefore they write.

Who write.

The human mind write.

What does the human mind write.

The human mind writes what it is.

Human nature cannot write what it is because human nature can not write.

The human mind can write what it is because what it is is all that it is and as it is all that it is all it can do is to write.

Yes that is right.

Of course it is right because and because and because that is why anybody can go on being able to read anything that has been written just as naturally as when it is or was written. If not why not.

There is no surprise in that. No surprise that writing can be read.

No surprise in that and yet not anybody says that that what anybody goes on reading is just that that which is not an event, Oh no, because nobody writes that. They write about weather and money, and weather and money have nothing to do with events or with human nature, they have to be the symbols of the human mind and the human mind is what it is and it writes that.

No one need have any doubt that there is no relation between human nature and the human mind.

There is none.

Chapter III

Just like a play.

Girls curl.
A grandmother uses napkins to make a dress.

Another Play.

But, But is a place where they can cease to distress her.

It is extraordinary that when you are acquainted with a whole family you can forget about them.

Another play.

It does not make any difference what happens to anybody if it does not make any difference what happens to them.

Program. She made a date with him which would not do.

Girls coming. There is no use in girls coming.

A man coming. Yes there is a great deal of use in a man coming but will he come at all if he does come will he come here.

Later when another man comes.

How do you like it if he comes and looks like that. Not at all later. Well any one he does come and if he likes it he will come again.

By and by. By and by is very fortunate it is partly what he takes and what he makes and very nearly partly what he does not hope that it will not do not do to do it after he does it.

What did they like. They liked partly liked everything which they needed very much.

There is no reason not to believe in the human mind.

PART IV

The question of identity

A Play

I am I because my little dog knows me.
Which is he.
No which is he.
Say it with tears, no which is he.
I am I why.
So there.
I am I where.

Act I Scene III

I am I because my little dog knows me.

Act I Scene I

Now that is the way I had played that play.
But not at all not as one is one.

Act I Scene I

Which one is there I am I or another one.
Who is one and one or one is one.
I like a play of acting so and so.
Leho Leho.

Leho is a name of a Breton.

But we we in America are not displaced by a dog oh no no not at all not at all at all displaced by a dog.

Scene I

The dog chokes over a ball because it is a ball that chokes any one.

He likes to kindly remember that it is not of any interest.

Part I Scene I

He has forgotten that he has been choked by a ball no not forgotten because this one the same one is not the one that can choke any one.

Scene I Act I

I am I because my little dog knows me, but perhaps he does not and if he did I would not be I. Oh no oh no.

Act I Scene I

A dog this time has choked by himself only the choke resembles a sneeze, and it is bothersome.

When a dog is young he seems to be a very intelligent one.

But later well later the dog is older.

Tears come into the eyes but not by blinking.

And so the dog roams around he knows the one he knows but does that make any difference.

A play is exactly that.
Here is the play.

Play I Act I

How are you what you are.
This has to do with human nature.
Chorus. But human nature is neglected.
Yes of course human nature is neglected as neglected as any one.
Chorus   And the human mind.
Chorus   And the human mind.
Nobody is told to close.
Nobody is told to close about what the human mind is.
And so finally so.
Chorus   There is no left or right without remembering.
And remembering.
They say there is no left and right without remembering.
Chorus   But there is no remembering in the human mind.
Tears.   There is no chorus in the human mind.
The land is flat from on high and when they wander.
Chorus   There is flat land and weather and money for the human mind.
And so tears are vacant.

And so sale and sale and sale is not money.
But money.
Yes money.
Money has something to do with the human mind.
Nobody who has a dog forgets him. They may leave him behind. Oh yes they may leave him behind.
And the result.
May be and the result.
If I am I then my little dog knows me.
The dog listens while they prepare food.
Food might be connected with the human mind but it is not.

Scene II

And how do you like what you are.
And how are you what you are.
And has this to do with the human mind.
Chorus   And has this to do with the human mind.
Chorus   And is human nature not at all interesting.

Scene II

Do you understand anything better through knowing where it is or not.
Chorus   Or not.
Chorus   No not because to know where you are you
         have to remember.
Chorus   Yes not.

Chorus. Of course yes not.
Chorus So of course nobody can be interested in hu-
man nature.
Chorus Nobody is.
Chorus. Nobody is interested in human nature
Chorus. Not even a dog.
Chorus. It has nothing to do human nature has noth-
ing to do with anything.
Chorus No not with a dog.
Tears. No not with a dog.
Chorus. I am I because my little dog knows me.
Chorus. That does not prove anything about you it
only proves something about the dog.
Tears. Yes there I told you human nature is not at all
interesting.

Scene III

And the human mind.
Chorus And the human mind.
Tears. And the human mind.
Chorus Yes and the human mind.
Of course the human mind.
Has that anything to do with I am I because my little
dog knows me.
Has that anything to do with how a country looks.

Scene III

Dogs and birds and a chorus and a flat land.

How do you like what you are. The bird knows, the dogs know and the chorus well the chorus yes the chorus if the chorus which is the chorus.

The flat land is not the chorus.

Human nature is not the chorus.

The human mind is not the chorus.

Perspiration is not the chorus.

Tears are not the chorus.

Food is not the chorus.

Money is not the chorus.

What is the chorus.

Chorus. What is the chorus.

Anyway there is the question of identity.

And that also has to do with the dog.

Is the dog the chorus.

Chorus. No the dog is not the chorus.

Scene II

Any scene may be scene two.

Chorus. And act II

No any act can be act one and two.

Scene II

I am I because my little dog knows me, even if the little dog is a big one, and yet the little dog knowing me does not really make me be I no not really because after all being I I am I has really nothing to do with the little dog knowing me, he is my audience, but an audience never does prove to you that you are you.

Act III

No one knowing me knows me.
And I am I I.
And does a little dog making a noise make the same noise as a bird.
I have not been mistaken.
Chorus. Some kinds of things not and some kinds of things.

Scene I

I am I yes sir I am I.
I am I yes Madame am I I.
When I am I am I I.
And any little dog is not the same thing as I am I.
Chorus. Or is it.
With tears in any eyes oh is it.
And there we have the whole thing.
Am I I.
And if I am I because my little dog knows me am I I.
Yes sir am I I
Yes Madame or am I I.

The dog answers without asking because the dog is the answer to anything that is that dog. But not I. Without tears not I.

Act I Scene I

The necessity of ending is not the necessity of beginning.

How finely that is said.

Scene II

Very much as everything is said.

Scene III

An end of a play is not the end of a day.

Scene IV

After giving.

PART IV

I wish very seriously were I I to have eight be an audience.

Do you mind eight.

What is the relation of human nature to the human mind.

Has it anything to do with any number.

The thing about numbers that is important is that any of them have a pretty name.

Therefore they are used in gambling in lotteries in plays in playing in scenes and in everything.

Numbers have such a pretty name.

It can bring tears of pleasure to ones eyes when you think of any number eight or five or one or twenty seven, or sixty three or seventeen sixteen or eighteen or seventy three or anything at all or very long numbers, numbers have such pretty names in any language numbers have such pretty names.

Tears of pleasure numbers have such pretty names.

They have something to do with money and with trees and flat land, not with mountains or lakes, yes with blades of grass, not much a little but not much with flowers, some with birds not much with dogs, quite a bit with oxen and with cows and sheep a little with sheep and so have numbers anything to do with the human mind. They have nothing to do with dogs and human nature but have they anything to do with the human mind, they ought to have something to do with the human mind because they are so pretty and they can bring forth tears of pleasure, but tears have nothing to do with the human mind not even tears of pleasure although they might all do so all do so and all be so.

Tears of pleasure have nothing to do with the human mind.

Chapter II

After all what is the human mind.

It is a very simple story.

The human mind is the mind that writes what any human mind years after or years before can read, thousands of years or no years it makes no difference.

Now human nature human nature is just the same as any animal nature and so it has nothing to do with the human mind. Any animal can talk any animal can be but not any animal can write.

Therefore and so far is the human mind not related to human nature.

And the writing that is the human mind does not consist in messages or in events it consists only in writing down what is written and therefore it has no relation to human nature.

Events are connected with human nature but they are not connected with the human mind and therefore all the writing that has to do with events has to be written over, but the writing that has to do with writing does not have to be written again, again is in this sense the same as over.

And so the human mind has no relation to human nature. And therefore and once again it is a ready made play to make a play of how there is no relation between human nature and the human mind.

A play.

It has been said that only human beings play games just as it has been said that only human beings have tears in their eyes but this is not so, dogs have dogs do, they stick out their tongue they turn their head away when their feelings are hurt and so there is no relation between human nature and the human mind.

And the land.

And any land.

The land has something to do with the human mind but nothing to do with human nature.

Human nature is animal nature but the human mind the human mind is not.

If it were then the writing that has been written would not be writing that any human mind can read, it has really no memory nor any forgetting.

Think of the Bible and Homer think of Shakespeare and think of me.

There is no remembering and there is no forgetting because memory has to do with human nature and not with the human mind.

Everybody says no when I say so but when I say so finally they do not say no.

A play of how they do not finally say no when I say so.

Act I Scene I

Myself. A dog is very much oppressed by the heat.

Scene II

Waking up is not the same as sleeping and have either

one anything to do with the human mind.

Act I Scene I

All this can if it does it can if it does not make a detective story or anything right away.

How does everybody feel to-day. Very well I thank you.

Act I

If the world is small how small is it.

If the world is big how big is it.

But if everybody knows what everybody does is it small and big.

Now listen everybody listen.

Everybody can listen and if everybody is dead it does not make any difference because there are so many more and everybody can listen.

Now this is Part one.

Part one.

Everybody can listen and that does not make any difference because no matter if everybody is dead there are always all the same just the same all the same anybody can listen.

But nobody does do this. Nobody does listen because everybody can listen and listen. Listen to that. What is that. And then they listen to that.

After everybody listens to that can nobody listen.

Not as much as before.
And after before.
Well after before anybody can listen
So once more a play.
But what is a play.
If there are no tears what is a play.
And if there are tears.
Where is a play.
Which and than have nothing more to do than just
nicely hear what every one can.
So now hear me say.
I almost cry.
Hear me say.
What is the relation of human nature to the human
mind.
Now there are two things that anybody can know.
A great many people do listen and a great many peo-
ple do write.
Now this is alright.
But after all where is it when the world is small.
Where is it it the world when the world is small.
Around and around and the world is small.
She complains and can the world become small.
Or not at all.
Finally a prayer has nothing to do with I care.
I can begin again so often that I can begin again.

If it were not possible to begin again would any one listen.

Oh yes of course no yes of course.

And now I am really not really but truly yes really and truly yes I am to begin again.

And is any one going to begin again. No yes not any one.

And so very few write because if to write and to begin again.

Why is it always that there is a beginning and a middle and an ending.

Because it is quite right that nobody can write.

Part II

This whole book now is going to be a detective story of how to write.

A play of the relation of human nature to the human mind.

And a poem of how to begin again.

And a description of how the earth looks as you look at it which is perhaps a play if it can be done in a day and is perhaps a detective story if it can be found out.

Anything is a detective story if it can be found out and can anything be found out.

Yes.

The human mind cannot find out but it is in it is not out.

If the human mind is in then it is not out.

Now in the first detective story the human mind does not count.

No. one. A detective story.

Detective story number one.

Do you remember no you probably did not read that part I remember because it is true not because I said it before but because it is so if it is so.

And so it is never necessary to say anything again as remembering but it is always said again because every time it is so it is so.

That is the difference between writing and listening.

When you write it is so when you listen it is not so because of course when you listen it is not so and when you speak well of course when you speak it is not so anybody knows that it is not so that when you speak it is not so.

And therefore there are strong silent men.

If not why not.

But anyway anybody can know that what you say is not so.

So what is so.

Anything is so that is so and that is what makes a detective story fascinating that if it were so it would be so.

I am going to write one.

Listen Detective story number I

If it is so is it so.

Or if it is not so is it not so.

But if you say so if anybody says so is anything so.

And if nobody says so is it so.

Is it so if you are writing. Yes it is so if you are writing because if you are writing how could you be writing if writing had not been learned. And so since it is learned since writing is learned it is so if it is written.

Now in talking well talking has not been learned so anybody talking is anybody talking and anybody talking has nothing to do with it being so.

How do you like a detective story if nobody is either dead or not dead.

You like it very well if it is written but if it is not written if it is not written everybody is dead.

Of course sometime everybody is dead but what has that to do with writing. Nothing at all. But with talking it has everything to do with talking. So you see talking has nothing to do with anything being so because everybody can come to be dead and so what is the use of saying that talking has anything to do with anything being so.

How I do like numbers this Detective story number one.

Detective story number I. About how there is a human mind.

And how to detect it.

Detective story number I.

The great thing to detect in a detective story is whether you have written as you have heard it said. If you do write as you have heard it said then you have to change it.

Suppose you have as a title Hub Murphy or the boy builder.

Supposing she says do not put in the or and then you try not to put in the or.

Do you succeed or do you not in not putting in the or.

And if you do why do you and if you do not why do you not.

The reason why has nothing to do with a detective story. They call it a motive but a motive is not a reason why. A motive is what makes you do it. But what makes you do it is not the reason why you do it.

Now this is not only true of detective stories but also of geography and government.

What makes you do it is not the reason why you do it.

Now listen a minute.

If you fly over Salt Lake city it is exactly like flying over the bottom of the sea with the water not in it.

The water is not in it, and so is there any reason why

the water should be in it. Sometime the water has been in it but now that the water is not in it it makes it more easy perhaps not to fly but to see what you see as you fly.

Now the reason for the water not being there is one thing but the water not being there is another thing.

Now suppose it is a detective story.

Well it is astonishing to see a pigeon where you had not expected ever to see one.

Not because a pigeon could not be there, not even because a pigeon had never been there but because you could never have expected a pigeon to be there.

Even the wind could not blow the pigeon away once it was really there where the pigeon is.

Then the pigeon almost falls off because suddenly there is another pigeon there and the pigeon had not believed it possible for another pigeon to be there.

Perhaps there is still another pigeon there but it can not be seen even if it is there and anyway the first pigeon turns his back so that he will not be able to see them or the other one and then he changes his mind and turns around toward them.

Perhaps from now on pigeons will always come there. Very likely because that is what anybody can do.

So once more no pigeons being there never again can there never be any pigeon there.

Detective story no. 2.

Suppose you know just what has happened does that make any difference if you tell it.

What is the difference between write it and tell it. There is a difference you can tell it as you write it but you can tell it and not write it. There is a difference and the next detective story is to detect that difference.

If the pigeon can come again and he has come again then he can surprise some one but he cannot surprise me.

A pigeon itself if anything is a surprise such as being there can be interested in anything being surprising.

Think how heavily a pigeon flies and alights and if he is there is he likely to think that the wind can blow him away. The wind does blow but does it blow as a surprise or anything to him. Has he a motive in being there and having been there does he come there again.

He does come there again and this has no connection with the wind blowing and there has been no motive for the coming there.

So then what does human nature do.

It does it because it does and having done it it is not because it has done it that it does it it does it because it is there again.

There they are again.

The three pigeons are there again. There is no reason

for it.

But if looking at it you are to paint it, the pigeon is there again and turning his back on the two other pigeons who are below it. You only can see from the side where you are seeing everything you only can see the two heads of the other two pigeons and now there are three. That makes four in all.

That is why numbers really have something to do with the human mind. That they are pigeons has nothing to do with it but that there was one and then that there were three and that then there are four and that then it may not cease to matter what number follows another but the human mind has to have it matter that any number is a number.

So then detective story number III

So then if then you might suppose then that if numbers mean anything there must be remembering. But not at all the number of pigeons being there is interesting as one follows one even if sometimes the one following is two or three, but you do not have to remember the one to know that there are two and three and all of a sudden four.

The minute you remember the one you do not want to look at him when they are one and then two and then four suddenly anything suddenly happening there is no remembering. Now think of how a detective story is to be written.

The first thing is the dead man or if not a dead woman.

No detective story can very often have a dead child or an alive pigeon because quite quietly anything that is begun is begun, and anything being finished is begun.

Mostly in detecting anything being finished is begun.

And so they prefer not to have dead children.

Any detective story is ready to be told. And as you know it you know it.

Detective Story number VII

Pigeons come to parties and when they come there is no reason that they come excepting that it is the first time that they come. If they have come they come as often as they come and when it is not comfortable then they are uncomfortable. Uncomfortable as it is it is as uncomfortable as it is and after that there is no reason why they have not come. In every little while an eagle can fly. That has nothing to do with any sky. Wait a minute.

Now this is how a detective story can be written.

I love writing and reading.

When there has been no rain the sky is very beautiful. Any one in America can know that and like it when it is heat producing.

Pigeons have nothing to do with this this has nothing

to do with several pigeons. Swallows flying in and out have nothing to do with any pigeon, flying in and out of a room. And so there is no such thing as human nature.

Why there is no such thing as human nature is that anybody can observe swallows and a pigeon.

There is blue and green and green and yellow pale yellow and blue, there is pale yellow and green and blue and warmth and there is not any such a thing as human nature.

Please see my human mind.

It is here.

Is white a color.

Yes white and grey is a color.

Grey and white is a color.

It is now come to be certain that there is not any such a thing as human nature.

Of course there is such a thing as human nature and anybody can observe it.

The relation of human nature to the human mind.

When anybody likes it as much as they ever liked it before they like it as much as that.

The detective story of liking it as much as they ever had liked it before.

They liked it as much as they ever liked it before because it was hot and they liked it to be like that to be hot.

They liked it as much as they ever liked it before be--

cause the wind blew and blew the birds about and they liked it they liked it as much when the wind did that.

Now how could you detect that they liked it as much as they ever liked it before.

Now here is where we come to this that having come to this they pushed every one with a chance to stay where they had been put but nobody had been put where they did stay.

And so after all why should pigeons come to stay because nothing that comes can go away because nobody has anything that has come to go away. And progress is just that, it has come to go away and so here we are now, and it is as hot and the wind blows nicely to-day and and any one finding that the dog went in when he was told said what did you say.

That makes a crime story what did you say if I had not waited to hear what you did say I might have said the wind is blowing to-day. And so a crime story as soon as you know what is what is what no crime story is. There is no such thing as crime and propaganda because nobody knows the difference between what did you say and what you did say.

What is what.

Very well I think that I think do not think which I do not think why I do not think just why this is that.

There is no crime, there is the hope that the daughter

of the couple could not be bitten and in order to do so they the couple are very careful.

And yet she might not be.

After all sometime she will not be older.

Not to the eye or to the ear but to circumstance.

And so hastily they vanish not hastily but slowly when they are no longer to stay.

That is just the difference between crime and no crime and there is no crime without crime. Who knows what.

I wish not to know but as I do know I do not wish to know what they do but I do wish to know what they do .but if I do then they do not do what I wish to know that they do. And so a crime story is ended because I look at the end.

Begin being ready to find the human mind.

Chapter V

Habit and the human mind is there any such a thing as habit and the human mind.

Do not be ridiculous of course there is not there is no such thing as the habit of the human mind.

The human mind if it is a human mind has not even the habit of being the human mind no of course not.

Detective story number 8

If wild animals live as if they were wild but they are

kept healthy and not killed are they wild. If they run away when they are seeing they are seen are they wild.

When anybody who knows where they are knows they are there are they wild.

Do you see how much all this has to do with communism and individualism and propaganda. But has it anything to do with the human mind.

Yes it has this to do with the human mind that the human mind may write yes yes or no or I guess I guess no or I guess yes.

The human mind cannot be interested in whether the animal which is wild is not wild but it can be interested in yes.

America the place where every animal is which has been there is interested in saying yes. No or yes.

The human mind if it rests in no and yes the human mind does not know about rest because no and yes have nothing to do with anything but no or yes.

And think, it is very exciting but think how much America and I do think America has something to do with the human mind think how much America has to do with yes.

Detective story number I

Will the world which is round be flat.

Yes it is.

When there was a sea the world was round but now

that there is air the world is flat.

Oh yes it is.

That is what a crime story is.

It is the human mind.

The human mind says yes it is.

In the years when nobody looked everybody said everything grows the same but it never does.

What if it did but it never does.

If it did there would be no human mind because no one could say yes if it always grew the same.

But it never does.

Now every one can but no one should get excited about it never does.

But since no one knows except the human mind that it never does that it never does grow the same that each year there is a little more or a little less rain, so then it never does grow the same.

Nobody is excited when it does when it does not grow the same but every one is excited when saying yes which is the human mind and which is the same says yes.

That is what makes politics and religion and propaganda and communism and individualism the saying yes and that is always the same and that is because it is the human mind and all the human mind can do is to say yes. Now do you see why there is no relation between human nature and the human mind. Human nature can not say yes, how can human nature say yes, human nature does what it does but it cannot say yes. Of course human nature can not say yes. If it did it would not be human nature.

Saying yes is interesting but being human nature is not interesting it is just like being anything and being anything is not interesting even if you can say anything because the only thing that is interesting is saying yes. Poor America is it not saying yes, is it loosing the human mind to become human nature. Oh yeah.

Part fifteen.

Four things that have nothing to do with this.

1. That when anybody is elected to do anything although he has never done it before he begins to do that.

I say to Upton Sinclair what would you have done if you had been elected and he said thank god I was not elected.

I used to wonder when I saw boys who had just been boys and they went into an office to work and they came out with a handful of papers and I said to them how since you never had anything to do with papers before these business papers were given to you how do you know what to do with them. They just did. They knew what to do with them.

And therefore that has nothing to do either with human nature or the human mind.

It is easy to see that it has nothing to do with anything and that most things have not, have not anything to do with anything.

There is human nature of course everybody has it and anybody can regard themselves or any one as having it but really it is not interesting. No not to-day since to-day well any day is nevertheless more yesterday than to-day and therefore not interesting.

When I say not interesting I mean not interesting.

A conversation.

If every one could go on living there would not then be room for any one now living.

Nobody says anything.

If every one could arrange what weather we are to be having every one would want what he wanted and what would that do, it would do nothing because if everybody had everything then everybody would go on living or nobody would go on living.

How do you like what you have can never be said of any one not of Theodore or Franklin Roosevelt not of Napoleon or Louis Napoleon. And yet inasmuch as that they are the same.

It is a funny question that if every one had everything they wanted every one would go on living and if every one went on living then there would not be room for any one and so nobody would go on living. Human nature even has nothing to do with this.

The human mind yes the human mind can say yes.

Human nature cannot say this human nature cannot say yes.

Moreover.

Theodore and Franklin Roosevelt like Napoleon and Louis Napoleon even though they belonged to the country to which they belonged were foreign to it.

This has nothing to do either with human nature or the human mind and one may say that neither of the four of them had any of them had any human nature or any human mind.

They could not be what they were that is human nature and they could not say yes that is the human mind.

They all four are very interesting examples of having neither human nature nor the human mind.

Theodore and Franklin Roosevelt Napoleon and Louis Napoleon.

I wish to make this absolutely clear because it is yes it is absolutely just as clear.

There is no age when she says yes.

If she says yes then there is no age when she says yes.

How pleasantly a doll can change its age.

But you know I know that if a boy is to grow up to be

a man what is the use.

Theodore and Franklin Roosevelt and Napoleon and Louis Napoleon.

Yes indeed everything is there nothing is missing nothing is missing to show that there is no need not to know that there is no human nature where there is a human mind.

Leave age alone.

I tell you leave age alone.

Leave forgetting alone.

Leave it alone.

I tell you leave it alone.

She said the child said well what did she say.

Theodore and Franklin Roosevelt and Napoleon and Louis Napoleon never said what they said was any more than led. They knew nothing of being dead. Of course not because they had no human nature. They said nothing of what was said no of course not because of course what is said is not said and they had no human mind to write what was not said. No of course not.

So this is to be a long story and let us play that it is a detective story only in a detective story somebody has had to be dead and these four no these four not as alive as dead no not not as alive as dead.

So a detective story if they cannot be dead well then perhaps there is a crime where not anybody is dead.

Well perhaps then something is said.

Of these four or not any more no they are not dead nor is it more than that which is said.

I leave well enough alone.

I Theodore Roosevelt.	As dead as not dead.
I Napoleon.	Not as dead as dead.
Louis Napoleon	Not at all as dead as said but dead as said.
Franklin Roosevelt.	Like Louis Napoleon oh very

much very much like Louis Napoleon. He has no commitment to dead and said.

Listen while I tell you more about all three or all four.

Sometimes it is all three because the two the two forget each other. Louis Napoleon and Franklin Roosevelt forget each other.

Whether they forget each other.

That makes two.

The other two do not forget each other.

Or at least.

No or at least if they are dead they are not not because of this may they be without date or dates.

They do not forget each other, they might then have human nature. They might but did they.

They never said what they wrote but they did not write.

As they did not write they did not have a human

mind. And they saw land they saw land oh yes they saw land but if they did, is it that they did, no if it as they did is what they did.

They saw the land they could use but they could not use land and as they could not use land they could see land but as they saw land what land well not any land because after all land is land, that is the human mind and they had no human mind.

At least not not at all they had no human mind and so there was no relation no relation between them and the land and so they are not dead and so what they said anything they said was not the human mind.

The human mind does not concern itself with what is said.

It does not concern itself with what is written. And they wrote nothing so nothing was written.

Of the four none of them having ever been existing no one of the four of them is dead.

So they need not rest in peace.

Peace is very likely something.

Has human nature anything to do with peace.

Not anything but something.

And has the human mind anything to do with peace.

The human mind has to do with yes and yes has nothing to do with anything and anything has to do with peace from time to time with peace.

Human nature only has to do with in between and in between oh yes in between sleep and peace oh in between.

And the human mind.

Part XV

The only difficulty about doing anything is that doing anything is nothing to do.

Nothing to do and doing anything is not the same thing because either one thing or the other thing is doing nothing.

Chapter XVI

Now just think of the meaning. Anybody just think of the meaning of not doing anything and think what all the government is and propaganda and money and individualism and collectivism, think what it all is is it doing nothing.

No not at all it is not at all not doing nothing.

Even Mr. Upton Sinclair cannot say no nothing at all.

But does he.

Yes he does.

He does say I see I see and any one can see I see I see.

There there there.

There is no way to quiet not not doing anything.

No other way.

They do not even forget not to have tears not Mr. Upton Sinclair although really and truly although he does not forget it he does not forget not to have tears.

That is what makes him Mr. Upton Sinclair.

Then very well what is the human mind.

If not if not what is the human mind.

Chapter one.

To know what the human mind is there is no knowing what the human mind is because as it is it is.

I could say something about history but although everybody likes to know about everything they think oh yes they think that when anybody is doing anything that is history.

Is there any difference between doing anything and something happening.

Quick and quickly as anything stops tapping is there any difference between doing something and something happening.

Of course there is.

Quickly of course there is.

And that tells all about history.

Nevertheless in bowing and listening and then the tapping is ceasing there is a difference between any one doing or not doing anything and anything happening.

This is the secret of history and it is not the secret of

human nature and the human mind.

Anybody doing anything may or may not have something in relation to human nature but certainly most certainly not it has not anything to do with the human mind because of course the human mind never does anything why should it, when it has no relation to human nature.

And so let well enough alone.

Now history has really no relation to the human mind at all, because history is the state of confusion between anybody doing anything and anything happening.

Confusion may have something to do with the human mind but has it.

I would rather not know than know anything of the confusion between any one doing anything and something happening.

So says the historian.

Chapter 91

The human mind.

There is no relation between human nature and the human mind.

Chapter 2

What is the relation of a calendar to the human mind even if one means to say an almanac.

An almanac has a relation to the human mind because every day it tells what it is.

An almanac has no relation to human nature because every day human nature tells what it was and therefore human nature cannot write but the human mind can.

It not only can but it does.

Chapter III

The question of identity has nothing to do with the human mind it has something although really nothing altogether to do with human nature. Any dog has identity.

The old woman said I am I because my little dog knows me, but the dog knew that he was he because he knew that he was he as well as knowing that he knew she.

Dogs like knowing what they know even when they make believe that they do not not that they do not like it but that they do not know.

Take a bicycle race that has nothing to do with a dog but it has to do with identity.

They are they because all who are there know they are they and on no account cannot they not be no not as long as they are in the race.

When they drop out well then identity may no longer be identity. They are they just the same only they are not because they are no longer identified and if they did not race at all well then not any one is any one.

All this has nothing to do with the human mind but so much to do with history and propaganda and government but nothing to do with money and the human mind nothing to do with money and the human mind.

Human nature, human nature acts as it acts when it is identified when there is an identity but it is not human nature that has anything to do with that it is that anybody is there where they are, it is that that has to do with identity, with government with propaganda with history with individualism and with communism but it has nothing nothing to do with the human mind.

Anybody can understand that because the human mind writes what there is and what has identity got to do with that.

Nothing nothing at all.

And so anybody can see that identity has nothing whatever to do with the human mind.

Just now when everybody knows that, think of crime identity has nothing to do with crime, detective stories yes but not crime.

Now to know to do as you do doing as you do has nothing to do with crime.

Chapter IV

It is beginning to be able to see that identity has

nothing to do with crime.

With the detective story but not with crime.

Chapter II

I am I because my little dog knows me.

That is just the way history is written.

And that is why there is really no writing in history.

I am I because my little dog knows me.

Yes that is what history is writing but not the human mind, no not, of course not, not the human mind.

Chapter III

The relation of superstition to identity and the human mind.

Please remember the cuckoo.

Chapter IV

There are so many things to say about the cuckoo.

I think I will say them all.

I have always wanted to talk about the cuckoo.

Chapter III and IV

About the cuckoo.

Long before the cuckoo sang to me I wrote a song and said the cuckoo bird is singing in a cuckoo tree singing to me, oh singing to me.

But long before that very long before that I had heard a cuckoo clock.

And in between I had heard a great many cuckoos that were not cuckoo clocks.

Indeed since then I have never seen a cuckoo in a cuckoo clock.

So then I did hear that a cuckoo not in a clock but a cuckoo that is a bird that sings cuckoo if you hear it sing for the first time in the spring and you have money in your pocket you will have it all the year. I mean money.

I always like to believe what I hear.

That has something to do with superstition and something to do with identity. To like to believe what you hear.

Has that something to do with the human mind that is with writing.

No not exactly.

Has it something to do with human nature. Well a dog likes to believe what he can hear.

You tell him what a good dog he is and he does like to believe it.

The cuckoo when he says cuckoo and you have money in your pocket and it is the first cuckoo you have heard that year you will have money all of that year.

It did happen to me so you see it has nothing to do with the human mind to believe what you see to like to believe what you hear.

But it did happen to me there was a cuckoo and he

came and sat not in a cuckoo tree but in a tree right near to me and he said cuckoo at me and I had a lot of money in my pocket and I had a lot of money all that year.

Now you see what a cuckoo has to do with superstition and identity.

Superstition is to believe what you see to believe what you hear and to see what you see.

That makes superstition clear.

And in a way yes in a way it has nothing to do with human nature or the human mind.

Superstition exists in itself because it is so true.

The human mind oh yes you do.

It is not concerned with being or not being true.

But superstition yes superstition is concerned with it being true.

And human nature human nature is not concerned with its being true.

And so superstition has nothing to do with either human nature or the human mind.

And that is very agreeable that it is that.

And now identity.

Well any Franklin Roosevelt has he any identity.

I am I because my little dog knows me.

But does any little dog know more than know that it is he.

No indeed.

And what is identity.

Is he he.

Does the little dog know that he is he.

But is he.

The little dog is like superstition he believes what he hears and what he sees and what he smells.

But is that identity.

Of course there are identity cards but is that identity.

Perhaps it might be just as easy to remember what identity is.

Perhaps to remember what identity does and if identity remembers them it has nothing to do with the human mind no nothing because the human mind does not remember it knows and it writes what it knows.

Now identity remembers and so it has an audience and as it has an audience it is history and as it is history it has nothing to do with the human mind.

The little dog knows that I am I because he knows me but that is not because of identity but because he believes what he sees and what he hears and what he smells and so that is really superstition and not identity because superstition is true while identity is history and history is not true because history is dependent upon an audience.

Oh yes oh yes upon an audience.

And this has nothing to do with the human mind.

And human nature well human nature is not interesting not at all interesting.

Chapter II

It is a remarkable thing not remarkable but remarked. Is there any difference between remarked and remarkable.

There are a great many people always living who are mixed up with anything and that is known as events.

But.

Only one sometimes two mostly only one sometimes none but certainly mostly only one in a generation can write what goes on existing as writing.

It is absurd when you think about it as absurd as any superstition but there it is there is only one in a generation not likely more than one in many a generation not even one that can write what goes on existing.

Now what have you to say to that.

That when you come to think about it it is astonishing but when you hear that there is no relation between human nature and the human mind it is no longer as astonishing.

How often as I have been walking and looking at so many who are studying and walking and I can say to myself why should not one of them write something that will be that that which it is and they will not no they will not and what is that that which it is.

It is writing of course it is the human mind and there is no relation between human nature and the human mind no no of course not.

And what has that to do with flat land or any land the flatter the land oh yes the flatter land but of course the flatter the land and the sea is as flat as the land oh yes the flatter the land the more yes the more it has may have to do with the human mind.

After number I

Number one I cannot be often enough surprised at what they do and that they do it so well, so much is written and they do do it so well.

And then I wonder as they do it so well as so many do it so many do it so very very well, I mean writing how is it that after all only one and that one only one in a generation and very often very many generations no one does it at all that is writing.

It has all to do with the fact that there is no relation between human nature and the human mind.

Those all those that do it so well and they do they do do it so well all those that do do it so well do it with human nature as human nature that is with remembering and forgetting.

Think anything you say has to do with human nature

and if you write what you say if you write what you do what is done then it has to do with human nature and human nature is occupying but it is not interesting.

No you all know you all know that human nature is not interesting, you watch any dog with affection no human nature is not interesting it is occupying but it is not interesting and therefore so much writing is done. But is it done oh yes of course it is done. Done and done. That is the way they used to bet.

Now you take anything that is written and you read it as a whole it is not interesting it begins as if it is interesting but it is not interesting because if it is going to have a beginning and middle and ending it has to do with remembering and forgetting and remembering and forgetting is not interesting it is occupying but it is not interesting.

And so that is not writing.

Writing is neither remembering nor forgetting neither beginning or ending.

Being dead is not ending it is being dead and being dead is something. Think of any crime of course being dead is something.

Now and that is a great American contribution only any flat country has and can be there that being dead is actually something.

Americans are like that.

No Europeans and so no European can ever invent a religion, they have too much remembering and forgetting too much to know that human nature is anything.

But it is not because it is not interesting no not any more interesting than being drunk. Well who has to listen to anything. Any European but not any American.

Number two.

That would be sad.

What.

That any American would hear what any one is saying.

Number three.

I found that any kind of a book if you read with glasses and somebody is cutting your hair and so you cannot keep the glasses on and you use your glasses as a magnifying glass and so read word by word reading word by word makes the writing that is not anything be something.

Very regrettable but very true.

So that shows to you that a whole thing is not interesting because as a whole well as a whole there has to be remembering and forgetting, but one at a time, oh one at a time is something oh yes definitely something.

Number four.

Why if only one person in a generation and often not

one in a generation can really write writing why are there a number of them that can read it quite a number of them in any generation.

There is a question.

Why do they as well as can they.

Number Five.

Do they as well as can they.

Number six.

One two three four five six seven all good children go to heaven some are good and some are bad one two three four five six seven.

So you see that this is the question.

How is it that a number a certain number in any generation can read what is written but only one in any number of generations can write what is written.

She dropped something.

Number six and seven.

Another thing.

What is the relation of anything to anything.

Not human nature and not the human mind.

Human nature is not that thing and the human mind.

Nor the human mind.

First Example.

The relation of the human mind to the universe.

What is the universe.

Human nature is not in any relation to the universe anybody can understand that thing.

That is not understanding that is unanswerable that human nature has no relation to the universe.

What is the universe.

Second Example.

There are so many things which are not the same identity, human nature, superstition, audience, and the human mind. And the only one that is the one that makes writing that goes on is the human mind.

Identity and audience.

No one is identical but any one can have identity.

And why.

Because what is the use of being a little boy if you are going to grow up to be a man.

Example Four.

Another thing that there is is the Universe.

Identity has nothing to do with the universe identical might have if it could have but identity certainly not certainly not identity.

Example Five.

Nothing should follow something because in this way there will come to be a middle and a beginning and an end and of course that does make identity but not the human mind or not the human mind.

If you write one thing that is any word and another word is used to come after instead of come or of come again then that may have something not to do with identity but with human nature.

And human nature has nothing to do with the human mind.

Now about anything nothing can grow but after all as nothing can grow there is no identity.

Not of course not even naturally not but just not, not at all.

But anything can grow.

But what is the use of being a little boy if he is going to grow up to be a man.

Do you see what a mistake it is to say that.

Example six.

The universe.

What is extra is not a universe.

No indeed.

Play I

Characters.

Identity, human nature, human mind, universe, history, audience and growing.

Play II

I do not think I would care about that as a play.

146

Play I

The human mind.
The human mind at play.

Play II

Human nature.
The dog if he is lost knows very well he will be found.

Human Nature.

But perhaps he will not be found.

Play III

Very often he is not found he is run over.

Play IV

Sometimes he is not run over but he is not found.

Play I
Identity.

If I know that I say that I will go away and I do not I
do not.
That makes identity.
Thank you for identity even if it is not a pleasure.

Play I

Identity is not as a pleasure.

Play I

Identity has nothing to do with one and one.

Play I
The Universe.
The Universe well if there is a way to have it be that they can lay a universe away.

Play II
But they cannot.

Play III.
Of course they can.

Play IV
Of course they can. They do not. But they can.

Play V
A universe if it is layed away, they cannot. Of course they cannot.

Play V
A universe cannot.

Play I
An audience.
An audience cannot be layed away. Of course it can. It can but is it. Of course it can.
Any audience can be layed away of course it can.

Play II
Growing.
There is no of course it can to growing.

Growing has no connection with audience.
Audience has no connection with identity.
Identity has no connection with a universe.
A universe has no connection with human nature.

Play I

Human nature.
Human nature is not interesting. Human nature is not a play.

Play II

Human nature is not interesting.

Examples seven and eight

The more likely a universe is to be connected with identity the less likely is a universe to be a universe.

No one likes the word universal to be connected with a universe.

Part II

All the parts are part II.
I once knew a man who never had part one he always had part 2.
I always knew.

Part III

Now what has any one to do with Part III

Part I

If every day it is necessary to have an uncle killed that

is if he kills himself instead of a father that too has nothing to do either with identity or with human nature.

Part IV

It is very strange that although only one in ever so often can write a great many can read what the one has written. But is that only because they can read writing or has it to do with the one who is writing.

That is what I want to know.

The human mind writes only once in a very little or big so often but every time every time size has nothing to do with anything because the universe every once in a while the universe is that size and so does it make any difference since the human mind has what it has does what it does and writes what it writes and that has nothing to do with identity or audience or history or events, and yet only once oh only once in every few generations the human mind writes. That is all because of human nature and human nature is not interesting everybody says it is but it is not.

Part I

He needs what he can please

Part I

Every time they change, I mean the earth I mean why mean the earth and which makes more than what is on it in it.

Part II
Once they like an earth

Part II
Once they like a heaven

Part II
Once they like a heaven and earth

Part III
No heaven

Part III
No earth

Part I
They come later not to know there ever had been a heaven.

Part III
Certainly it lasted heaven a very little time all things considered that is considered as long as anything is.
No earth yes no earth.
No heaven yes certainly no heaven.

Part III
Now this which I want you to think about is this.
Every once in so often is every once in so often and anybody can decide what nothing is.
Please excuse me.

If nothing is anything any one every once in so often can decide what anything is.

That is the way it is.

Part I

Every time there is a human mind it is or it is not all the universe which is or is not.

That is what the human mind is.

Think what the human mind is.

Part II

It has nothing to do with anything but is one yes well yes that is what the human mind is.

Part III

Is one yes that is what the human mind is.

Part IV

Human nature no.

Human nature never is one that is not what the human mind is human nature is not what the human mind is.

Part IV

Romance.

There is some relation between romance and the human mind but no relation between human nature and romantic anything because human nature is not interesting but romance is.

Part I

Lolo.

Part II

I cannot begin too often begin to wonder what money is.

Has it to do with human nature or the human mind. Human nature can use it but cannot refuse it. Can human nature know it know what money is or only the human mind and remember now there is no heaven and of course no earth, not in America perhaps not anywhere but there is the human mind and any one which is more than not enough may perhaps know what money and romance is.

Part I

I am not confused in mind because I have a human mind.

Part II

Yes which is.

Part I

Romance and money one by one.

Part II

Lolo.

Part II

Care fully for me.
As often as carefully.
Each one of these words has to do with nothing that is

not romance and money.

Part III
Romance has nothing to do with human nature.

Part III
Neither has money.

Part I
Lolo.

Part II
Where he lived and when he died.
Some see some sun.

Part III
He died naturally

Part I
She says he says he says she says what is done is not done.

Number one.
It is not to discourage to say that each time although each time is such a very few times that there is a different way to say that the sun is far away each time that there is a different way to say that anything is far away although at any time that there is a universe now at any time that there is a universe anything is very near.

Number two.
That is just that and that has nothing to do with the

human mind or human nature that is just that.

Number one.

It happens it changes a little any day it happens though that any day some one can say something that makes any one know that the larger is smaller but not that the smaller is larger.

Now suppose everybody says pioneering is over that means that the larger is smaller but not that the smaller is larger and that well that no that that has nothing to do with the human mind.

But has the human mind anything to do with romance not human nature perhaps human nature. Who likes human nature. Not I. And the human mind. And romance oh yes I do like romance that is what makes landscapes but not flat land.

Flat land is not romantic because you can wander over it and if you can wander over it then there is money and if there is money then there is the human mind and if there is the human mind there is neither romance nor human nature nor governments nor propaganda.

There should be none of these if the land is flat.

Flat land as seen from above.

Above what.

Above the flat land.

Is there any human nature in red indians or chinamen

there should not be.

But there is.

Alright there is.

But there should not be.

Is there any romance.

All right there should not be.

But there is.

Alright there should not be.

And government, no there is no government where the land is flat.

There should not be.

And there is not.

And why not.

Because anybody can wander and if anybody can wander then there should not be any human nature.

And romance

No there should not be.

And yet romance has nothing to do with human nature.

No nothing.

Nothing at all

Nothing at all.

Nothing at all at all

Nothing at all.

Number II

Lolo.

There is no romance if anybody is to die by and by.
But to die
Yes to die.
Not only not to die.
Not by and by.
And so romance is delicious.
But not to die by and by.
Lolo.

Number three.

Lolo was one no matter that he had a father.
No matter that he had a father.
Nobody cries out loud no matter that he had a father.
It was not mentioned often or again.
Lolo was himself romantic and he is dead not by and by but dead.
And as I pass where he had not had a father there where he is not dead by and by but as he is then there there where he is he was not where he is. Lolo is dead and any father had a mother he had a mother but none of this is dead.
He is dead.
Lolo is dead.
There where there is no other.

Number III

Do you see what romance is.

Number III

Do you see that it has nothing to do with human nature or the human mind.

Number III

So many things have nothing to do with human nature.

Romance did.

It had nothing to do with human nature.

And the human mind.

Nothing did.

Nothing did have nothing to do with the human mind.

Romance did.

Oh romance did.

Romance had nothing to do with the human mind nor with human nature.

Romance did.

Number III

It has to do with neither with flat land or money or the human mind or human nature.

Now anybody might think that romance and adventure was the same but it is not.

Adventure has to do with small things being bigger and big things being smaller but not romance no not romance. Romance has nothing to do with anything being bigger or being smaller and therefore although romance has nothing to do with the human mind they come together.

They have nothing either one of them has nothing to do with human nature. Oh no nothing to do with human nature.

Lolo.

Nothing to do with human nature.

Number I

Every time any one can come to be one then there is no human nature no not in that one.

Human nature has to do with identity but identity has nothing to do with any one being one.

Not not anything in any one.

No no no.

Number II

Be a credit to beware.

Does it make any difference how you felt to-day.

No not any

Does it make any difference how you felt yesterday

No not any.

Does it make any difference if a dog does not know the difference between a rubber ball and a piece of paper.

No not any why he does.

Ah there you see.

That is the answer.

No not any only he does.

Now that has to do with identity.

Does it make any difference if a dog does not know the difference between a rubber ball and the end of a rug.

No not any only he does.

In this way identity is proclaimed.

Not of the ball and the rug but of the dog.

So you see I am I because my little dog knows me.

But that has nothing to do with romance but it has to do with government and propaganda.

Oh yes you do see.

You do see me.

And that has to do with government and propaganda but not with money and the human mind.

Oh yes you do see.

But do you see me.

That has to do with human nature but not with romance and money and the human mind but with government and propaganda and human nature and adventure, oh yes you do see you do see me.

Number III

Very nearly any is as much as not nearly as much

more.

Quantity is one of the things to think about and how much do you use.

She complains that some who do not live on flat lands do not know how much of anything they use.

What has this to do with money. Nothing at all really and now I will explain all about money.

How do you do all about money.

Money is what they know that they give and take.

Oh yes yes.

Number IV

Four and five do not keep money alive any more than six and seven.

Now just think they do say at sixes and seven.

Number V

Money is very important because anybody can think about that and it has nothing to do with the human mind.

And with romance.

Well and with romance.

And with big and little no not with adventure and with human nature.

Human nature can mix itself up with it but that is another matter. Really money really has to do with the human mind.

Part VII

What did swallows do before houses were built as they do not care for trees.

Part VIII

This has nothing to do with romance because the mention of it is bad.

Bad which is badly has nothing to do with sad, and all this both has nothing to do with romance.

Romance has to do with what it looks like.

It looks like near and far this is not adventure it is romance, romance has to look like near, adventure has to look like far, and to adventure is to bring the far near, romance is to have the near far and here.

How likely are definitions to be pleasurable.

Very likely.

Part IX

Define what you do by what you see never by what you know because you do not know that this is so.

Autumn can come in June but very soon it mostly can come in July.

You see why romance is interesting and not adventure.

Every once in a while anybody can say so.

Part X

I think that if you announce what you see nobody can

say no. Everybody does everybody does say no but no-body can nobody can say so, that is no.

That is the reason that you can say what you see
And do you see.

That is what the national hymn says the star spangled banner.

Oh say can you see.

Part XI

Everything is funny that is nothing at all.
But the human mind.

The human mind believes in a glance and also in looking.

Even so.

Part XI

Now I wish earnestly to say just what I see when I look away.

That is one thing.

Earnestly to say what I see when I look any way.

Earnestly to say what I see as I see that I look to see.

Sometimes it is very beautiful like to-day.

Oh yes sometimes like to-day.

Any day is neither here nor there.

Let no one think that anything has come to stay.

And if they do if they do not think that anything has come to stay what is the difference between to-day and any other day.

But there is a difference.

There is no use in saying there is no difference because there is a difference there is a difference between to-day and any other day.

There is no need of their being any difference no need at all.

Now do you begin to see the difference between need and is, between human nature and the human mind and of course you do see why it is not interesting to any one who has need to be that is who finds human nature interesting.

Oh dear human nature is not interesting.

Part IX

Romance is not interesting but it is made at once made at once by where they are.

Oh where they are.

Yes nobody needs to know about yesterday and to-day if they are where they are, and the only way to be there where they are is by romancing.

Romancing oh not that romance makes where they are there.

It is the only thing, history cannot do it nor government nor propaganda nor human nature nor the human mind.

Romance is the only way to be there there where they are.

So romance is in between human nature and the human mind but has nothing to do with either.

Detective story the story of a dead man should have had a connection with romance because a dead man if he is really dead but only in America dear America the United States of America is a dead man really dead.

And so that is romance do you see because a dead man there is dead and dead is dead there. Not adventure, adventure is just hurrying the distant to be nearer, but romance romance is to be there there where they are.

Not described as that to that but to be that not described as that.

I wonder if you could be cured of not knowing that.

It really makes it be us to be like it is.

And the human mind. The human mind has to say what anything is now. Not ever where anything is that is romance but has to say what anything is now oh yes yes yes that is the human mind.

Part XXI

I should be liking to love swallows so.

The human mind. Oh yes I know.

Human Nature.   Oh yes oh yes.

Romance.   Oh yes this is yes.

Adventure.   Which is yes for the mess swallows
can know.

Government.   Yes swallows yes.

Propaganda.   Oh yes.

Part XIII

I believe I do not like anything that happens.

I believe I do not like what is not alike.

I believe I do not like where the air is there.

I believe I do not like while they like.

But a swallow let something tumble upon me from the air.

Part XIV

This was missed as seen.

Part XV

I believe that I like to see what is seen.

Ah yes of course.

I believe that I like to see what bothers me.

Oh yes of course.

I believe that I like to be what is not human nature to be because human nature is not interesting.

Oh no decidedly not. I believe that human nature is not interesting. Decidedly not.

But anything flying around is.

Oh certainly.

Therefore there is the universe.

Because it is flying around.

It is interesting.

Anything that is flying around is interesting.

Human nature government propaganda is not flying around adventure is not flying around, it is flying to or from therefor it is not interesting.

And romance and the human mind.

Well and romance and the human mind.

Romance and the human mind are interesting and are they flying well no they are not.

So there we can say that only the things flying around are interesting which makes the universe, and flat land and romance and the human mind but perhaps they do and perhaps they do not fly around romance and flat land and the human mind, of course they do they do fly around. Moving around is not flying around the things that move do not make the universe. They are not interesting.

The human mind is interesting and the universe.

About romance well supposing we just like it like that but not by definition.

But wait we will define it so that it is interesting. Nobody can define events or history or human nature or government or propaganda and make them interesting. Anything that has to do with human nature is not interesting.

Just think.

How very uninteresting human nature is. If you like it like that what is the matter with the dog the two dogs both of them asleep.

They are sweet but not interesting once you know that human nature is not, not interesting.

Number I

Now is just the time to think about what is or is not interesting because nothing else is interesting.

Everything else is as well finished as begun everything except to find out what is or is not interesting.

Leave well enough alone means nothing now because nothing is alone.

That is it.

Not even the human mind.

No nothing is alone.

And if nothing is alone then every one can know that nothing is alone and so no one can leave well enough alone since nothing is alone.

And so you see there is nothing to be except the universe and the human mind and is the universe alone and the human mind.

Can leave well enough alone be said of the universe or of the human mind.

I wonder very much where there is.

So does no one.

If any one is alone and everybody is then nobody is alone as nobody is.

And so nobody can leave well enough alone.

How happy it is to be exact but to be exact is to be happy.

Happy is not exactly as it is and since nobody is alone nobody is as happy as it is.

So romance has nothing to do with anything excepting only as it looks like it as country.

Country not flat country can look like something.

The human mind does not hop around but it flies around and is alone as the universe is.

Therefore nobody but it writes it, and that makes it the human mind that it writes it.

Part I

I should not have ended as begun.

If anything flies around there is no ending and no begun.

Part II

I am coming to what the human mind is and I have one.

Part III

One.

Part IV

The human mind has not begun it happens once in a while but it has not begun.

Part V

Will it

Part VI

No.

Part VII

Money.

Part I

Money is a very interesting subject.

Part I

Franklin Roosevelt like Louis Napoleon has no personality but a persistence of insistence in a narrow range of ideas.

Money and personality.

Two things which may or may not be connected with human nature and the human mind.

For all of which there is praise and no praise.

Part I

Money.

Part I

Personality.

Part I

Money very likely money has nothing to do with human nature.

Human nature makes me smile.

Smile with what.

With what I smile.

But money, money is not just the same not at all just the same.

Part I

I wish seriously to talk about money.

Part I

Personality, personality has nothing to do with money or with the human mind. Nothing at all.

And human nature well human nature can always let well enough alone and so human nature well human nature can never be alone but money can money can be alone and it is best it is alone money is alone and the human mind and the universe.

Part I

There can be a union.

Part I

Money is alone.

Part I

You learn it in writing poetry you tell it in writing

prose.

This is even true of politics.

Sadism is an entirely different matter.

But is it.

If it is is it.

Sadism may have something to do with human nature and the human mind.

There are connecting links not in arithmetic but there are connecting links so they think in zoology, but I never think.

Sadism is no connecting link but it may have something to do with either not something to do with but is something that has something something to do with human nature and with the human mind and although no one can separate anything from sadism sadism cannot live alone. But the human mind. Well can it.

We have talked so much about time and identity that now we really know it know that we can see that one can make three.

To Thornton and Bob Davis an autobiography.

Autobiography I

When I was one that is no longer one of one but just one that is to say when I was a little one, but not so little that I meant myself when I said not one.

When I was that one, I said that when I was looking

I did not see what I was seeing.

That can happen to any one.

Of course it does. Be natural and of course it does.

You are looking you are seeing what you are seeing and are you.

If you are one then now and then you are not that one. That can happen at any time. It does happen when any one is a little one and any one, any one is then one.

So you see time and identity mean what they say when they say that they are not existing.

Be natural oh yes do be natural and do have what you have, and if you have what you have then you do not have time and identity inside in one since you do have that when you are looking you are seeing what you are seeing but perhaps not.

Really that has really nothing to do with anything.

But what has.

That there is no identity and that there is no time.

What is the use of being a little boy if you are going to be a man.

Which is which.

Autobiography number II

I tried in Making of Americans to make any one one. How.

By having a beginning and middle and ending.

But is there any such thing as a beginning. Be natural

is there.

And a middle.

And an ending.

Any one who is one can be natural if he can. If he cannot he can be just as natural as he can that is within his human mind, and in his human mind he never did begin, he never has begun he never began.

Of course not if he did where is he.

Anyhow there is nothing the matter with this.

And so human nature is not in any way related to the human mind.

Nobody need be triumphant about this.

Think of the master-pieces remember how few there are and how many anybody is. And so why be happy and yet anybody is.

I wish writing would not sound like writing and yet what else can any writing sound like.

Well yes it can it cannot sound like writing because if it sounds like writing then anybody can see it being written, and the human mind nobody sees the human mind while it is being existing, and master-pieces well master-pieces may not be other than that that they do not exist as anybody seeing them and yet there they are.

Please please me.

Anybody can please me, but that is not what the human mind is.

Sadism no that is not what sadism is.

I am not confused but belated, can the human mind be belated.

I like words that have been left alone and words that have not been left alone.

Which of these is belated.

Autobiography number III

To see everything as flat.

That not being autobiography but the history of master-pieces,

Is the history of master-pieces autobiography.

Autobiography number II

Seeing everything as flat.

When you look at anything and you do not see it all in one plane, you do not see it with the human mind but anybody can know that. It is naturally that. And so it is because there is no time and no identity in the human mind.

The human mind has always tried to say that of something else but why when there it is right in the human mind. That is because the human mind can think that human nature may be what it is but human nature is what human nature is which is not the human mind.

The human mind has neither identity nor time and when it sees anything has to look flat. That is what makes master-pieces makes a master-piece what it is. And when it is only that only no time or identity then it is that.

Yes we can say that naturally of course naturally naturally it is that.

Autobiography number I

I noticed to-day under a tree nobody was singing to me there they were just as they were but they did not look as if they were flat, so they were not a master-piece no indeed not.

Autobiography number I

Anyone can read any one who is one and very often it is master-pieces it is the master-pieces that they read.

They read them and they are one the master-piece is.

There is no identity and no time in a master-piece nor in the human mind.

No of course not.

It is the habit to say that there must be a god but not at all the human mind has neither time or identity and therefore enough said.

Be natural and anybody who has a human mind and anybody who has has will know this.

If anybody is natural they know what is.

It is what it is.

Least said soonest mended but a great deal is said.

You say I say he says, but I have not expressed a part at any time.

No not at any time.

Autobiography number one.

Could there be a time when all the time the human mind was within which time.

No not at all.

Because there would then be more master-pieces or there would not then be all the time then any one then who knew the master-pieces of any time when then they had them.

I remember so well always saying in the Making of Americans then knowing not knowing but having then the difficulty of being sure that then was then.

Any one can have that inside them and therefore then well then then is what they say again and again but not then.

Do you see how sweetly I can be having then not then.

Oh yes I know then when then is not then.

But it never is because there is no time and no identity in the human mind.

It is so natural to know this thing that everybody does so naturally know this thing that anybody would naturally know this thing if they did not believe what they saw although naturally anybody can know if anybody can tell them so that they do not believe that they saw what they saw.

That is why superstition is so sweet.

Of course it is sweet.

It is just as sweet as sweet as it can be.

I believe what I know although nobody tells me so, because I know that I believe what I know. But in doing so, there is no time in me and no identity.

Autobiography number V

When I was at college I studied philosophy that was it they did not know what they saw because they said they saw what they knew, and if they saw it they no longer knew it because then they were two.

It is just as necessary as that and that is why a young one knows it too, he knows he is through not because he is young but because he is through.

Of course he is through with philosophy because just then he is not yet two.

The minute you are two it is not philosophy that is through it is you.

But when you are one you are through with philosophy, because philosophy has to talk to itself about it, anything but a master-piece does that and if it does then it is not one but two.

You see that is what religion means when it says two in one and three in one and so religion can try to be one in one. But not really one because then it is not yet or ever begun.

So though they say it is one they try to make it as two.

So after all then even in religion one is not one.

But in the human mind and in master-pieces oh yes oh yes.

Autobiography one again.

It is not I who doubt what it is all about but she says clearly, human nature is not only uninteresting it is painful but I it is not I who doubt what it is all about but naturally what it is is what it is not.

Time and identity and what is it that the human mind does and if it does it what does it do it about.

Identity.

I knew him that is I have known him and it has always been the same him the same hymn, it has been the hymn of having his pictures within.

Yes and so when they said he was divorcing I could not believe that it had been done by him but it was because the pictures not inside him but the pictures outside him were being taken away from him. The pictures inside him even if they were being taken away from him that is changed inside him were still the pictures that there were inside in him.

Now this might mean that there is identity if you were to say that this is so which it is but nevertheless there it is not because to-day is never to-morrow or yesterday although if it is if to-morrow is to-day that is what she can say she can say that if to-morrow is nearer to to-day, so some can say so she can say then to-morrow is to-day but if to-morrow is not anywhere near to-day which is what he can say then to-morrow cannot be to-day.

Yesterday nobody can take any interest in because there is not really any of any such a thing.

So once as once and not once again because again and again is not anything identity and time is not any confusion. Natural enough is natural enough.

Let me tell the history of my life the life which makes any identity not be away because there is no identity that is not there to stay.

What is it.

Naturally when inside is inside it sees outside but it is inside.

Therefore identity and time have nothing to do with from time to time since inside is inside even if it does see outside.

I began with this.

Yes Miss I began with this. Only two ses are not the same as one.

But what is the same. He acts the same. Does that

make identity one and one and one.

But certainly not because otherwise there would be a use in being a boy if you are going to grow up to be a man and there is none.

Autobiography number one.

Anything can make me think what money is, what is it.

No one can know that any one can know that not any one is troubled so that they cannot be careless.

I was not careless about identity and time oh no I was not and I was not no I was not careless about romantic scenery no I was not, and if I was careless about money no I was not I was and I was not that is what money is I was and I was not about money and I was careless about sadism and if not then why not, sadism is not interesting if not so once when then is about sadism an if not then we do not count it as interesting. Money is interesting and romanticism not human nature and sadism. Make it another thing if you like sad is and sadism. Do you see what I mean very likely yes and that is not interesting even though anybody can enjoy reading which very often is just what makes reading like sitting and sitting and running is not interesting although very occupying and filling. Oh yes who likes to include gardening what is the difference between gardening and farm-

ing. Money is the difference and money who likes money money is what we all agree, to be happy and make
money, is anything.

But now why should not it be likely that farewell is
spoken.

Farewell if it is spoken should be romanticism and
has romanticism time and identity think about that.

Inside in any human mind there is not there is no
time and there is no identity otherwise what is inside is
not. But if it is inside then there is not there is no time
and there is no identity. But romanticism and money
which has to do with what is what and what is not what.
What is what is money, what is what is not and yet what
is not what, that is romanticism which is not what not.
Romanticism which is what. Answer me that which is
what.

It is not a flat surface romanticism like the master-
pieces and yet it is because it is so thick that yes it is. If
something that is not flat is thick enough then it is that
it is flat. And so romanticism can be a master-piece. But
sadism well you can see that sadism can never become
flat because it never can become one. Romanticism can
when it is thick enough. And money yes when it is thin
enough to be all that money is which is what it is. Thick
or thin wide or dim left to him taken to win, winning is
a description of a charming person.

Autobiography number one.
I am writing all this with an American dollar pen.

Autobiography.number one.
What did I study I studied philosophy and science and psychology and medicine and I read literature and history, and any other thing that can make reading.

And what happened while I was doing all this well anything if you like well anything but mostly if you like anything. Now I can have liked to tell it as a history of finding out about anything that there is no time and identity inside in me that is inside in anything and that there is no use in leaving well enough alone because by and by well because there is no by and by. Because mention me if you can because I am here.

Why need you think you can believe about a dog because you love him. You can love a dog and you can not think about anything which is kindly enough.

It is wonderful how a handwriting which is illegible can be read, oh yes it can.

Autobiography number one is almost done.

Autobiography number one
Not solve it but be in it, that is what one can say of the problem of the relation of human nature to the human mind, which does not exist because there is none

there is no relation, because when you are in the human mind you are in it, and when you are in human nature you are of it.

Become Because.

Beware of be.

Be is not what no one can be what no one can see and certainly not what no one can say.

Anybody can say be.

Be is for biography.

And for autobiography.

No not for autobiography because be comes after.

So once more to renounce because and become.

When I was certain that science was stating what any one was seeing and human nature well I was going to be stating anything that any one could be seeing and human nature was that thing, I was writing the Making of Americans. But supposing yes one did see anything and there was time enough time did not make any difference because there is always time enough, if there is enough of anything then one need not be worrying and there always is time enough. I then no longer was worrying about time but I just stopped going on. That is what time is. There is always enough and so there is no going on no not in the human mind there is just staying within. That is a natural thing when there is enough of anything and there always is enough of time. So then time is nothing since there is always enough of it.

The human mind has nothing to do with time since it is within and in within enough has nothing to do with anything.

Oblige me by not beginning. Also by not ending.

But human nature oh yes human nature always has to do with enough.

That is you might say all human nature does it does do with enough.

But autobiography which has no be in it demands of me that I say that the day that I knew that there was time enough to say all that was so of human nature then I did not do so any more, because anything that you see is so and the master-pieces which just are not master-pieces are always telling as so. Of course it is if it is so but the human mind oh no it is not so.

The human mind is not so because being within it has nothing to do with identity or time or enough.

Anybody knows this as a natural thing, just begin with within that is do not begin, no do not do not begin, how can any one begin when within is not cannot be begun. Just be reasonable about this, please just do. It is so simple to have it be true. Oh yes these are ordinary ideas.

But then, philosophy and science and medicine.

Philosophy tells why nothing is begun but if it is not

begun then there is no why. Inside anybody inside anybody inside knows there is no why to not begin because there is no such thing. No such thing as begin.

Human nature is not natural it is what anybody does and what anybody does is not natural and therefore it is not interesting.

There is no doubt that human nature is not interesting although the human mind has always tried to be busy about this thing that human nature is interesting and the human mind has made so many efforts always it is doing this thing trying to make it be to itself that human nature is interesting but it is not and so the masterpieces always flatten it out, flatten human nature out so that there is no beginning and middle and ending, because if there is not then there is no doing and if there is no doing then there is no human nature and so to do without human nature which is not interesting is what within the human mind is doing.

There is no relation between the human mind and human nature.

Each one is as it is.

Philosophy tries to replace in the human mind what is not there that is time and beginning and so they always have to stop going on existing. There are consequently practically no master-pieces in philosophy.

Philosophy then says human nature is interesting.

Well it is not. That is all that there is to say about that. It is so easy to be right if you do not believe what you say.

Please listen to that.

Autobiography number one now almost completely begun.

Avoid be in begun.

It is so easy to be right.

If you do not believe what you say.

Of course there is believing what anybody else can say.

Of course there is nothing in that.

Religion has been called natural.

Well there is something in that, because religion does know that there is no time and no identity and no enough and no human nature in the human mind, but religion is timid and so it does not say why or how but it does say where and saying where it must look over there.

So little by little which is not enough I found that enough is not enough and not enough should be treated roughly.

So finally I became so attached to one word at a time even if there were always one after the other.

Now then let me tell the story of my life.

The story of my life.

Chapter one.

At that time I had no dogs

Chapter II

So I was not I because my little dog did not love me. But I had a family. They can be a nuisance in identity but there is no doubt no shadow of doubt that that identity the family identity we can do without.

It has nothing to do with anything if there is no time and identity. But it has to do oh yes it has to do with how do you do you do do what you do.

The human mind lives alone.

That is the way you feel in Chapter II

Chapter III

Master-pieces are there they always have been there but do they make identity for you.

They do not make time that is certain and identity one can then be tempted into changing them into identity.

But if one does.

No one does what they do.

Chapter II

You identify yourself with master-pieces in Chapter II and in chapter three they give you identity, but in Chapter one none there is no identity and no time and in Chapter IV anybody can shut any door.

If you can shut any door identity has no meaning that is what happens in Chapter four.

Chapter IV

Move around quickly and then stop completely is what is happening in chapter four.

Chapter four has no identity and no time and more than all there is of enough. Enough said.

Chapter IV

So anybody can see that is to say it is natural enough it is ordinary enough that there is no identity and no time and no interest in enough.

After that there are many hours of occupation and master-pieces are master-pieces.

This is one's life from birth to sixteen and the rest is not worth while recording master-pieces I mean.

Master-pieces and identity.

If it is natural if it is as seen is seeing naturally what is seen.

There is no use in being discontented with what anybody sees.

But master-pieces, no master-pieces are not there but everybody says that is what a master-piece does but does it. Does it say what everybody sees, and yet it does but is not that what makes a master-piece not have it be that it is what it is.

Think are master-pieces natural enough and what is natural enough.

Master-pieces and identity, audiences and identity, do these separate to please or do they not do as they please.

When the little dog wants the ball he forgets to get it if he does not please and if he does and does get it then is his identity an audience. It looks as if it is but is it.

A master-piece certainly has nothing to do with identity because identity if it had an audience would not care to be a master-piece.

Not leaving anything alone is not what a master-piece does.

But really what I would like to know is why the very good things everybody says and everybody knows and everybody writes are not master-pieces I would really very much like to know why they are not. And when I say identity is not yes there is something in it all the time that there is not.

If not why not.

So many words to use.

Oh do not say that words have a use.

Anybody can tell what everybody knows but what does that disclose.

Oh dear what does that inclose.

After all what everybody knows is not a master-piece but everybody says it is.

Do they.

Oh yes everybody says it is.

But everybody knows what everybody knows.

And human nature is what everybody knows and time and identity is what everybody knows and they are not master-pieces and yet everybody knows that master-pieces say what they do say about human nature and time and identity, and what is the use, there is no abuse in what is the use, there is no use. Why not.

Now listen. What is conversation.

Conversation is only interesting if nobody hears.

Hear hear.

Master-pieces are second to none.

One and one.

I am not frightened but reasonably secure that whether it is so whether it is so whether it is so.

Master-piece or none.

Which is one.

I ask you which is one.

If he had not been frightened away he might have drunk at water but he finally did.

This is as good an example of a master-piece as there is.

Page I

Play for he and its thorn.
So music can replace nature.
But what is nature.
Not music
Music only can replace nature.
What is nature.
Nature is what it is.
Emotion is what it is.
Romance is what it is and there can be no romance without nature.
But is nature natural.
No not as natural as that.
He reads master-pieces but he knows nature and music is not that.
An ode to Thornton.

Page I

I meant to do just what I do but I never meant to do just what if I do I do.
Is that just human nature or the human mind.
It is neither.
Is it money.
Yes perhaps it is money.
Let us linger upon money.

Volume I

Money is what words are.

Words are what money is.

Is money what words are

Are words what money is.

There can be no romance without nature, there can be no money without words.

There can be nature without words.

Nature is here used in the sense of natural scenery and what land is.

And so nature is not what money is.

There can be music without words.

So there can be no music where words are.

Therefore music has nothing to do with money and with words.

Did I say embrace the problem no neither embrace nor replace the problem.

But to accustom oneself to the problem the problem of why if human nature is not interesting are master-pieces supposed to be interesting because of the subject of human nature in them.

Of course they are not the master-pieces are not because the human nature in them the telling of human nature in them is the same telling of human nature of those that do not make master-pieces by the telling of the same things about human nature that the master-pieces tell in them.

Human nature is not interesting and what the master-pieces tell about human nature in them is not what makes them everlastingly interesting, no it is not.

They read master-pieces, I read what are not master-pieces but which quote pieces of master-pieces in them. And what do I find I find that comparisons and human nature is not what makes master-pieces interesting.

But money and a word and romanticism.

They they have nothing of any human nature in them.

And thank you for not.

Money and words and romanticism have no time or identity in them, oh please certainly not.

Get used to them, you cannot get used to money or words or romanticism no certainly not.

But you can get used to human nature, yes certainly that.

Anybody can get used to human nature.

You see the only thing about government and governing that is interesting is money. Everything else in governing and propaganda is human nature and as such it is not interesting. Everything else has time and identity which is human nature and that is not at all interesting. No it can be completely understood that the only thing that is interesting in governing and government is money. Money has no time and no identity and no human nature, because of course it has not.

Let us remember how what happens happens.

Nothing happens.

Page II

Words. Very well. Words.

What are words.

Any word is a word.

There is no use to say accustomed.

All words are not words to which you can get accustomed or used.

Therefore a great many of them cannot go into master-pieces.

Those to which you can get used or those to which you cannot get used.

Cannot or can get used.

Any word which can go into a master-piece is one to which you cannot get used or perhaps not.

Anyway what is a master-piece. There is no doubt of what is a master-piece but is there any doubt what a master-piece is.

I like to be kindly.

I like to forget.

I like to make old horses be mules.

I like oxen to have wealth.

I like cows to be nearly able to feed.

I like to look about me.

I like to have no animation.

I like birds to have gone away.

I like arrangements to be made.

I like a chance to burn leaves.

I like what they understood to be clearly.

I like it when it turns up.

I like it by nearly alone.

After all why may it not be true that every one knows this.

They do.

But why may it nearly not be true that it is not difficult to do.

It is not difficult to do.

In the first place think of words apart or together.

It makes anybody happy to have words together. It makes anybody happy to have words apart. Either may not have anything whatsoever to do with human nature.

Any word may and does not have anything whatever to do with identity too.

Nor with time.

There are no tears when you say and not with time.

Nor either when you say not with identity.

It carefully comes about that there is no identity and no time and therefore no human nature when words are apart.

Or rather when words are together.

Beginning and middle and ending gathers no pleasure, and no money and no romanticism and no human mind.

When the piece of the master-piece is quoted, a very little at a very little time does any part come apart.

No because it has never been together never been other than together.

Either that or never apart.

Identity is very curious.

Not even the dogs can worry any further about identity.

They would like to get lost and if they are lost what is there of identity.

They would like very much like at all to get lost.

Lost.

That is what you say. Lost.

They would like to get lost and so they would then be there where there is no identity, but a dog cannot get lost, therefore he does not have a human mind, he is never without time and identity.

Poor dog how he would like to be lost.

They make believe that they would like to go out of their mind and so be lost.

Poor dog who is not cannot is not lost.

Let me tell you a story.

Basket a story.
Interlude I

I am I because my little dog knows me.
Is he he when he does not know me.
This sometimes happens.
That is his not knowing me.
When it does not happen he sometimes tries to make it happen.
So is he he when he does not know me.
And when he does not know me am I I.
But certainly this is not so although it really very truly is so.

Page III
Identity

Thank you for a name.
Thank nobody for the same.

Identity

Is it well to know the end of any identity.
Supposing you begin well and do know quite as well that you are you.
When you are you say it and when you say it you know it if by knowing it you can say it.
I say that spoken words mean nothing, written words yes because by the time they are written they are no longer said.

Anybody thinks about writing that is not written to anybody knows this.

The words spoken are spoken to somebody, the words written are except in the case of master-pieces written to somebody, somebody somebody there is the identity that of somebody. Somebody tears come to my eyes when I say somebody, and why well because the word sounds like that that of something like a dog that can be lost. Anything that can be lost is something anybody can get used to and that is identity.   .

And so in the human mind which can write but not speak, which can write but not get used to what it can write can write but cannot get lost, that is what the human mind is.

I do not know whether or not human nature can get lost but it certainly can get used to it and so it has its identity.

Do I make this clear, hear oh hear do I do I make this make this clear.

To hear.

I wish it were easy to say what a master-piece is as to say what human nature and time and identity is.

Anything that is or can be lost is so easy to describe because it is of no interest.

But money.

Well money is not easy to describe. It is easy to lose

but it cannot be lost, and no one can get really get used to it.

And romanticism.

Nothing is there when he says he likes music better, which means not at all that he does not like what he likes at all. Not at all.

Page IV

Bob Davis.

What is human nature.

If you please you do not know.

But you do not have to know because never to refuse is never to excuse and so well not at all and so.

You need not expect time to be solid.

You might but you do not have to.

And as you do not have to you do not.

Do not have to.

You do not.

So Bob Davis.

What do you do.

Nothing.

And why not.

Because there is no time.

Quite naturally not.

And Bob Davis why is natural not the same as naturally not.

If it is solid it is naturally not.

That is it is not naturally not.

There is no confusion in solidity rejoining.

Bob Davis may not be a pair.

Because identity is not there.

At a distance we saw a man on a bicycle and at a distance he looked like two.

There is no need to measure.

There is no solidity where there is a measure.

And so identity is not a ball, no not at all.

It is not there.

Where.

Where is it not there.

Anywhere.

Bob Davis.

Wherein a master-piece is not a thing.

There is no in within.

By the time I know what a master-piece is.

Well.

By the time I know what a master-piece is.

Page IV

Human nature is so not interesting that there is not any of a different thing in there being no time and identity.

Page IV

Plainly not identity as much as plainly identity.

Human nature plainly worries about identity.

And so human nature is all of identity and who is who.

If they asked who is who what would identity do.

Page two.

I said once I said perhaps it is true that what makes poetry possible is a small country. Big countries cannot really make poetry because they do not cannot all when they say the same thing feel as they do.

By this I mean.

All this I mean.

Page two.

Now when I said this did I mean that poetry is what is seen.

Suppose I do mean this.

Poetry may be what is seen and it often is.

Poetry is not identity no that it never is.

Poetry may be time but if it is then it is remembered time and that makes it be what is seen.

And so poetry a great deal of poetry is what is seen.

And if it is then in so far as it is it is not a master-piece. What is seen may be the subject but it cannot be the object of a master-piece.

But a great deal of poetry is made up of subject and if it is then it is not a master-piece.

In a small country where the land is not flat and where as you look you see what it is if it is as it is a great deal of poetry can and will and shall and must and may be written.

And that is as it is because anybody saying anything anybody knows what it is.

But in a large country and even in a small one if it is flat not every one can see what it is when they see what it is.

It is because of this that so much poetry of what it is that is seen is written in a small country that is not flat and that can go on to do what it has to do.

But in a flat country it must have content but not form and that may make a master-piece but is it poetry.

Master-pieces master-pieces there is no use in asking where are you because that everybody knows but what are you well that may be nobody knows.

Well anyway poetry is poetry and a great deal of poetry says what is seen as it is, says what it is as it is seen. Yes.

Page nine.

I know the difference between what is and is not that is I know the difference between what it is and what is it and in doing so have I come to go that is to know which is it.

Like this.

203

Like this is not to like this.

Any word is a word that they use and in America where the land is flat they do see that there is no use in there being any use in knowing what it is because is it is it what it is.

They do not glow because they think it is so and so they do not know that it is so in other words as likely as not it is neither what or why it is so since not at all is never said no not in America.

What have master-pieces to do with what is never said or indeed with what is said.

Nothing at all either gradually or not at all.

Now listen to this.

If a master-piece is what it is how can then its not being one effect it.

All that is silence because it makes longing and longing and feeling have nothing to do with what a master-piece is.

Occasionally nothing to do with what a master-piece is.

Even if it is a feeling of longing it has nothing to do with what a masterpiece is.

Thornton Wilder what is a master-piece.

He says he hopes he knows that longing has nothing to do with what a master-piece is.

With which they wish that longing has nothing to

do with what a master-piece is.

I do I know what has nothing to do with what a mas-ter-piece is.

They say longing has to do with what a master-piece is but they are mistaken longing has nothing to do with what a master-piece is.

I said to Basket my dog look and long but I said this has nothing to do with what a master-piece is and he may not believe it he easily may not but it has not does not have anything to do with what a master-piece is.

Page I

They like to remember to forget and that that is this has nothing to do with what a master-piece is.

Page I

What is a master-piece and how many of them that is are them.

Well believe it or not it makes no difference to them.

Page I

I would kindly not like to know what a master-piece is.

Page 2

About detective stories is the trouble with them that the one that is dead has no time and no identity for him to them and yet they think that they can remember

what they do not have as having it without their having
it for them.

I would like to read a detective story every day and
very often I do.

Page II

I think nothing about men and women because that
has nothing to do with anything.

Anybody who is an American can know anything
about this thing.

Page III

How completely I know and I tell you so that it has
nothing to do with men and women nothing to do with
anything anything with anything that is with anything
nothing to do with anything.

After all nothing to do with anything with like that
nothing.

Men and women may not regret human nature just
as they like they may not regret anything.

Has anybody neglected the human mind.

I have.

What you have.

In this way have is what you have.

I can never neglect have at least not for very long because in it without it is all there is of master-pieces and
the human mind. Because have is just that word.

Page IV

I could admire what I have just said.

Page V

I resist the temptation to say it again.
And so kindly allied.

Page I

They never had any.

Page I

I can slowly change to what I say.

At Page I

Well well at page one.

Finally it is true that soldiers who are not at war look as they do.

Is that so.

Any word will do.

Therefore it is true

That any way you see it is what is where they have it and yet all knitting if it is done by hand can and does resemble that done by machine.

And any one is deceived and only those that are interested make use of it.

What is a master-piece.

Any one that is no one is deceived because although any one can quote it no one can make use of it.

It is not any loss to lose a master-piece.

Every once in a while one is lost.

I remember very well deciding not to worry even if a master-piece should get lost. Any master-piece ancient or modern because there is no such thing as ancient or modern in a master-piece how can there be when there is no time and no identity.

And if a master-piece is lost then there is just one less to know about and as there are so few after all does it make any difference.

Suppose you have them all or none at all

But nevertheless master-pieces do have to have existence and they do each one they do although there are very few.

We know very well that master-pieces have nothing to tell how can they when after all anything that tells what every one tells tells what any one tells.

I tell you that any soldiers at all look as soldiers are.

Of course they do.

Anybody too.

And master-pieces do only master-pieces have to be what they tell well anybody can tell anything very well.

Shakespeare

I said to Thornton Wilder but you do know that the psychology in Shakespeare is no psychology at all. A young man whose father was just murdered, would not act like Hamlet, Hamlet was not interested in his father, he was interested in himself, and he acted not like a young man who has lost a loved father but like a man who wants to talk about himself, that is psychology if you like but anybody in any village can do that.

Now in a master-piece what does anybody do they do what they do that is they say what they know and they only know what they are as they know what they are, there is no time and no identity, not at all never at all ever at all.

Page I

What is the difference between conversation and writing, oh yes what is the difference the difference is that conversation is what is said and what is said is always led and if it is led then it is said and that is not written. Written writing should not be led oh no it should not be led not at all led.

And so writing is not conversation. Also then there is the fact that human nature is not scenery that land which is seen is not announced. Human nature is announced it announces itself it says yes I did it before but scenery well scenery if it did before does it now but human nature if it does it now did it before.

Scenery if it did it before does not remember but human nature if it did it before does remember because everything that human nature does it does remember

and if it remembers it then it is not interesting and if it
is not interesting then it is human nature. The only
thing about human nature that holds the attention is
that it has a beginning and a middle and an end and
when a book is not a master-piece it is that which de-
termines it that it has a beginning and a middle and an
end, the middle is mostly not as interesting as the beginning and the end and that is because it is not based
on human nature but it is human nature and therefore
not a master-piece.

Now scenery has no beginning and middle and end,
and that is what makes scenery romantic. If it had a beginning and a middle and an end as a storm has then it
would not be romantic, the storm is romantic because
the scenery is there and the scenery had not a beginning
and a middle and an end.

Now that makes master-pieces easier, not easier to
do but easier, and the human mind.

Also it makes romanticism easier, never forget there
is also money.

Also there is why is it that in this epoch the only real
literary thinking has been done by a woman.

Yes please think of something.

That is it.

Please think of something. And so no need of going
around, because the scenery is there, not a storm, sol-

diers are not a storm, they look like it they look like not a storm, if anybody salutes you and respects you that is like a storm, and so in this epoch the important literary thinking is done by a woman.

But yet yes.

By no means cease.

Page II

Romantic and romanticism, it is a pleasure to all beholders that a landscape is there and as it is there, what is there to see of it, only that which is not human nature, even a storm.

A storm would like to have a beginning and a middle and an ending, but very likely it settles as well.

Really settles has no need of triumph and yet that is just what a storm does and so it is not human nature. Human nature and triumph they would hardly like that. Which they hardly would like.

Human nature is not interesting some say triumph is.

A storm is romantic like a storm is but human nature is not like a storm because human nature does not act like that it only acts like a storm when it knows about a storm and when it knows about a storm it acts like a storm.

Has that anything to do with master-pieces.

It has nothing to do with human nature.

Forget human nature when it is human nature.

There is no use in forgetting scenery when it is scenery because there is nothing to forget.

Once more I can climb about and remind you that a woman in this epoch does the important literary thinking.

And money what is the connection between romanticism and money and master-pieçes.

Which one is it.

There never is a which one.

Page I
No one would if they could relieve page one from page one.

Page II
It is an obligation to have money connect itself with romanticism because that too is not human nature but scenery and if there is a storm then insofar as there is a storm there is triumph.

Page II
After all war in war is no different than war not in war except that there are more dead.

If there are more dead is there a difference and if there is a difference has it to do with money and romanticism.

Nobody criticises what is not war by what is not war.

And yet after all there is no difference when there is a difference and when it is all neither war nor more war.

And so they fairly evenly place it where money is.

And when there is no money at all does he know what money is. More money is not what money is.

Do you see its connection with romanticism.

A little gradually not at all, in among not as more than all.

Bennett would like another portrait.

What is a portrait to him.

A portrait to him.

What is it.

A portrait to him.

Page III

Human nature has nothing to do with it.

Human nature.

Has nothing to do with it.

Page IV

Emptying and filling an ocean has nothing to do with it because if it is full it is an ocean and if it is empty it is not an ocean.

Filling and emptying an ocean has nothing to do with it.

Page IV

Nothing to do with master-pieces.

Page V

Nothing to do with war.

Page VI

War has nothing to do with master-pieces.
Who says it has.
Everybody says it has.
Does anybody say what a master-piece is.
No nobody does.

Page VIII

So then the important literary thinking is being done.
Who does it.
I do it.
Oh yes I do it.

Page XXI

Money one.
Romanticism one
Scenery one
Human nature not one.
Master-pieces.
Human nature never knows anything about one and
one.

Page XXI

Storms.
Even a little one is not exciting.

Page XXI

Is there any difference between flat land and an ocean a big country and a little one.

Is there any difference between human nature and the human mind.

Poetry and prose is not interesting.

What is necessary now is not form but content.

That is why in this epoch a woman does the literary thinking.

Kindly learn everything please.

Page XXII

How ardently hurry comes too late.

That is what they used to say

Donald.

Donald and Dorothy Dora and Don Donald and Donald he comes when he can.

If he can when he can as he can nine.

Donald and Donald is all in one time.

To-morrow is as Donald would say twenty a day.

What does Donald do.

He does it all.

Of course what does Donald do.

Of course he does he does do it at all.

Donald dear.

Welcome here.

If he comes yes he comes.
Yes he comes.
If he comes.
Any Donald is not Donald there.
Donald there is not any Donald here.
But better here.
What if Donald may.
Not likely is not as different as very likely.
And very likely Donald is here.

Page XVIII
I may not be through with Donald.

Page XIX
Donald has nothing to do with romanticism.
Donald has nothing to do with money
Donald has nothing to do with scenery.
Donald has nothing to do with human nature.
Donald has nothing to do.
Donald.
No one can reproach Donald.
Donald and Dorothy and once there was an ocean and they were not drowned.

Page 2.
You.

Page III
Why should a woman do the literary important lit-

erary thinking of this epoch.

Page IV
Master-pieces are what they are.

Page V
There is no identity nor time in master-pieces even when they tell about that.

Page X
Is Franklin Roosevelt trying to get rid of money. That would be interesting, but I am afraid it is only human nature, that is electioneering and that is not interesting.

But it would be interesting to try to get rid of money by destroying it and if it could be done it would be interesting.

Why would it be interesting.

Because perhaps money has to do with the human mind and not with human nature. Perhaps like master-pieces it concerns itself with human nature but it is not related to it, oh yes yes.

Could one get rid of war by it becoming like duelling and would the way be by stopping saluting, if nobody saluted and nobody received saluting and nobody saluted and nobody wore any clothes that were given to them would that have anything like duelling to do with war ending, oh yes oh yes, and has war anything to do with the human mind no it has to do with human nature because it is not like money it might be like romanticism but is it, it might be but is it.

If it is yes is it.

In the nineteenth century when they wanted it to be a mystery it ended with the dead man in the twentieth century when they want it to be a mystery they begin it with a dead man.

And in plays well what are plays.

Do not listen to some.

What are plays.

A play.

It begins with a dead man a dead woman and a dead dog but they are not dead because the play goes on.

If the dog is dead does the play go on.

If the army is dead does the play go on.

If the dog is not dead does the play go on.

No indeed no certainly not.

Play 2

If the dog is not dead and the play does not go on is the man dead.

Yes the man is dead.

If the man is dead and the play does not go on does it go on. Yes it does go on.

If the woman is dead and the dog is dead and the

man is dead does the play go on.

Certainly not the play does not go on.

What does it mean.

Certainly not the play does not go on.

Does it mean it does not go on the stage.

Certainly not it does not mean certainly not not on the stage.

And so there is no time and no identity please be careful not to surprise tears.

In the nineteenth century they did not surprise tears they dwelt with tears because the man and the dog and the woman were not dead when anything began in the twentieth century everything that is any one is dead when it can and did when it began and so there are no tears were no tears.

Play I

Now how can they come to be now.

Play I

Any little thing is how it was begun.

It is clearer than any one that there are no tears now.

Play one.

Alright play one.

Play two.

It should be two to be through.

But there is that.
That as it has not to be that that is not that.
It easily is.
More and more a master-piece is.

Play III

I begin to see see I begin but there is no begin not in not in.

Play IV

Do you see it is to be.
But there is be as well as see.

Play V

So then

Play VI

The glory of knowing what a master-piece is.

Play VII

It is natural that again a woman should be one to do the literary thinking of this epoch.

Chapter I

I have it as quite that a master-piece where it is there.
To-morrow it will be warmer to say so.
So there is no need to be free.
They say so but there is no need to be free.
Did I say so that perhaps Franklin Roosevelt is get-

ting rid of money but perhaps he is only electioneering.

Anybody can know that human nature is not interesting and now not even necessary.

Not even necessary.

Chapter III

I so easily said it would be interesting and cried to have it interesting and be and may be I do but I doubt it not interesting.

I have made no intention.

I tell him content without form, lizards without homes and there should be a third and as there is there is a beginning and middle and end.

But content without form.

Who has hoped to be hoped.

I tell you it is true that I do the literary thinking for you.

Even perhaps if Franklin Roosevelt wants to get rid of money.

Chapter II

It is just as necessary not to have any human nature.

Volume II

Why was Polonius the one to say the things he said in his advice to his son because of course any one who writes anything is talking to themselves and that is what Shakespeare always has done, he makes them say what he wants said just then and he can make any one that one.

Ordinarily anybody finishes anything.

But not in writing. In writing not any one finishes anything. That is what makes a master-piece what it is that there is no finishing.

Please act as if there were the finishing of anything but any one any one writing knows that there is no finishing finishing in writing.

Perhaps Franklin Roosevelt wants to get rid of money by making it a thing having no meaning but most likely not most likely it is only electioneering.

What is money and what is romanticism it is not like human nature because it is not finishing it is not like a master-piece because it has no existing.

Very likely that is what it is money and romanticism.

And all the time was I right when I said I was losing knowing what the human mind is. Anybody can know what human nature is and that it is not interesting. Anybody can begin to come to know what money and romanticism is.

Master-pieces have no finishing in them and what anybody can say is what anybody can know and what anybody can know is what anybody can see but human nature and war and storms have a beginning and an ending as they begin they end and as they end they be-

gin and therefore they are not interesting and money
and romanticism they do not end and they do not begin
but they do not exist and therefore they are not anything although any one can feel that way about them
and therefore although they are not anything they are
interesting.

Marionette

Is a marionette a Punch and Judy show and suddenly how to know that Punch and Judy are their names.

When I have said that I know everything and in saying so explain everything at any time of all that time it is
as well said as it is said that I know everything.

There is no use in not knowing everything since certainly and knowing most most may not be must but
there certainly is the knowing everything.

Of should never be introduced and really it is no
temptation not to introduce of.

Of knowing everything.

More than likely knowing everything is what is
happening.

It comes back to must.

If there is must then there is not the knowing everything.

Knowing everything comes when in explaining everything there is the knowing that more often there is the
knowing everything.

Why are they inclined to leave must alone.

Because must is must.

So much for must.

And knowing everything is never left alone.

In knowing everything never being left alone there makes a recognition of what mater-pieces are.

Knowing everything is never left alone nor is it ever without being knowing everything. Anything else is of no account. Not in mater-pieces.

Knowing everything well everything you know is knowing everything very likely everything in master-pieces. But never ever anywhere.

There is no where in knowing everything, did we say no time and no identity well and then no place. Space is not interesting because if there is no place there is no space but space is there, well how about money and romanticism nobody wants to know about that.

Space and money and romanticism.

Leave master-pieces alone do not annoy them although they like if they like and they do like romanticism and money and space and they like to look at storms and war and human nature although they do know that they are not interesting.

Knowing everything is interesting. Oh yes yes.

A little play.

War and storms.

Romanticism and money and space
Human nature and identity and time and place.
Human mind.
Master-pieces.
There need be no personages in a play because if there are then you do not forget their names and if you do not forget their names you put their names down each time that they are to say something.
The result of which is that a play finishes.
How often does anybody like to leave before a play finishes.
Has that anything to do with master-pieces.
Not if you know everything
Oh yes not if you know everything.
Knowing everything does not remind everybody of something and yet it just might.
And if it well if it did then it just might.
I certainly do know all about knowing everything.

Volume I

Identity
In case of there not being any possibility of remembering and therefore no way of not losing what is not there where you are is there any way of enfeebling imagination. Indeed what is imagining anything. Is it done a little at a time or is it done a whole at a time and is it

done all the time.

They like to know why there is a question and answer. There is in detective stories but is there in real life. Is it possible to imagine a question and an answer.

You never answer a question nobody does.

So then is there in anything a question and answer. And what have master-pieces to do with this thing with their being no question to answer and no answer to a question.

If one is never right about anything and nobody ever is. Anybody who likes can know that, that really they are never right about anything. The more you are right about anything you never are right about anything it does not make any difference. It is only in history government, propaganda that it is of any importance if anybody is right about anything. Science well they never are right about anything not right enough so that science cannot go on enjoying itself as if it is interesting, which it is. Why not if it is. Human nature not we have come to not thinking that being human nature is interesting enough so that it can go on enjoying itself. Human nature as human nature no longer enjoys itself enough to be enough. And master-pieces have always known that. They have also always known that being right would not be anything because if they were right then it would be not as they wrote but as they thought and in a real master-piece there is no thought, if there were thought then there would be that they are right and in a master-piece you cannot be right, if you could it would be what you thought not what you do write.

Write and right.

Of course they have nothing to do with one another.

Right right left right left he had a good job and he left, left right left.

Vol II

How little need there is to be as right as to have it be Volume two but it is volume two and volume two is not volume two.

Volume two

I have been writing a political series just to know as well as to know that I am always right that is I am always right when I say what I say and I always say something that is what I am doing I am always saying something but as I am never writing what I am saying when I am writing I am as it were not saying something and so then there it is that is what writing is not saying something content without form but anyway in saying anything there is no content but there is the form of question and answer and really anybody can know that a question if there is an answer or an answer if there is a question is almost always almost human nature which we do know we are not right about it but we do know it know that it is not at all interesting.

It is so easy to know what is not interesting that is it is so easy to know it as it is not interesting. And yet anybody can say that may be it is not so. Of course it is so. Would I not be right if it were not so because it is so.

Just so.

There is no reason that a succession of words should spoil anything when it is always a pleasure.

Human nature is not a pleasure.

Volume III

A Play in which there is not only question and answer but identity.

Imagine that he always liked to write what he says.

He always does.

Does he stop himself when he always does. If he does not stop himself when he always does then he always does. Is that human nature or a master-piece.

Once in a while an individual looks as if he knew what identity is. He does not stop himself not to know what identity is.

Question and answer is so nearly not any more than a pleasure.

And it has no identity.

Question and answer has no identity it has only a form.

If they like to know that they know how pleasant a question and its answer is need they stop themselves from going on. Not at all, they nearly as well do not stop themselves at all from going on. That is what a question and answer is.

Even if there is no pleasure in it that is what a question and answer is. And might there not be any pleasure at all in it. Well yes and no not exactly.

In a way there always is a pleasure in it and there is it like romanticism and money has it something to do with what is not human nature with place and time in itself. In the human mind there is no identity and place and time but in money and romanticism and question and answer a little something yes that is not human nature but has something that is space and time and identity.

Human nature has nothing it is not interesting.

Page I

Do I do this so that I can go on or just to please any one. As I say it makes no difference because although I am always right is being right anything. No it is like human nature it is not interesting and therefore I can ask do you not get tired of always being right but there is something so much more pleasing and that is what is what. And what is what is what is what.

Do not remember question and answer although there is no use in forgetting because question and answer is like romanticism and money. Now we have all this there.

Page I

What is a play.

A play is scenery.

A play is not identity or place or time but it likes to feel like it oh yes it does it does wonderfully well like to feel like it.

That is what makes it a play.

A novel is something else it depends upon its liking to feel that human nature is interesting and therefore there is a middle and a beginning, in a play there is none, but a novel knows that human nature is not interesting and it purposes that if it were it would have a middle and a beginning and a middle and a beginning need not necessarily have an ending, therefore in a really good novel the ending is where it is but a novel is middle and beginning and therefore human nature asks as it does although really human nature has no middle and beginning and so a novel really knows that human nature is not interesting.

Now that is a play and a novel, now essays poetry philosophy and history and biography.

Every once in a while is not every once in a while because it does happen so rarely.

Volume II
If I want to find a volume I number it differently.

Volume III
If you believe what you hear do you believe what you
read and what is the difference between what you read
and what you see.

Have master-pieces anything to do with what you see,
no because what you see is as if it were there. And where
is it. It is there. Therefore when you read about it as if
it were there then it is not a master-piece.

And you do so often read about it as if it were there.
I do all the time and is there any difference if you read
about it as if it is there and its being there. If you hear
about it as being there then it is not really there not as
there as when you read about it being there, but seeing
it be there is not more than reading it being there. All
this has so much to do with master-pieces that it is
always necessary to read some more.

Its being there has nothing to do with question and
answer with romanticism and money. Has it anything
to do with master-pieces. It almost has if it has. Now
and then a master-piece can escape any one and get to
be more and more there and any one any one who can

write as writing is written can make anything be there again and again and that is what is so exciting about a detective story, they can make it be there again and again, oh yes any little part of it again and again and so are all detective stories master-pieces how much would anybody like to know that. Not any more than that. It has to be very well known this has to be very well known not to be known and as yet by me it is not well enough known yet not to be known.

Anybody likes it to be known that it is real when it has been written.

What is real when it has been written, it does not have to be a master-piece oh dear oh dear oh dear no. Human nature has nothing to do with this so I believe.

If I write slowly I would write as slowly as this.

It is getting very difficult to be there. Anybody knows how easy it is for anything written to be real. Not when it is almost anything but when it is anything oh yes a detective story or any easy novel oh yes and to some something is real and to some nothing is real that is written but writing can make anybody cry. Yes indeed yes. It is so difficult to have anything have anything to do with master-pieces.

Yes Thornton.

Volume II

I have met master-pieces when I was young.

As young as young.

And master-pieces when I was young.

I have met master-pieces.

If a thing can be read again does it have to be remembered.

Anything that is anything can be read again.

And anything seen.

And anything heard.

Do you know any differences.

Volume I

I am I because my little dog knows me. The figure wanders on alone.

The little dog does not appear because if it did then there would be nothing to fear.

Volume II

I liked the difference between being alone and not alone.

This made her surrounded.

Now in a master-piece neither one of these is so.

There is no possible doubt that what human nature does has nothing to do with it nothing to do with being alone or not alone because either one of these things is that.

Not that it is no not at all.

Very likely a master-piece is all of and only that.

Do you like identity because then acquaintance is not begun.

Very much as they like the same detective to appear again. And yet they wish that it was not. Because if it is it is expected and if it is not it is not unexpected.

Identity then is not at discretion.

I so easily see that identity has nothing to do with master-pieces although occasionally and very inevitably it does always more or less come in.

It is not known that anybody who is anybody is not alone and if alone then how can the dog be there and if the little dog is not there is it alone. The little dog is not alone because no little dog could be alone. If it were alone it would not be there.

And so a little dog cannot make a master-piece not even now and why.

And yet by recognising that the little dog would not be there if it were alone it can be that I am I because my little dog knows me comes into a master-piece but is not the reason of its being he.

What difference does a master-piece make if there is no dog to be. No dog can be alone. Can a master-piece be alone. Well they say so but is it so.

So then the play has to be like this.

The person and the dog are there and the dog is there and the person is there and where oh where is their identity is the identity there anywhere.

Every century not every century nor every country not every country has what they know is not identity.

For this nobody has to be thankful.

The only relation between anything is master-pieces and master-pieces therefore never have anything to do.

Identity not being the same not even in name, it is so evident that identity is not there at all but it is oh yes it is and nobody likes what they have not got and nobody has identity. Do they put up with it. Yes they put up with it. They put up with identity.

Yes they do that.

And so anything puts up with identity.

A dog has more identity when he is young than when he gets older.

When he is young a dog has more identity than when he is older.

I am not sure that is not the end.

Library of Congress Cataloging-in-Publication Data

Stein, Gertrude, 1874–1946.
    The geographical history of America ; or, The relation of human nature to
the human mind / Gertrude Stein ; with an introduction by William H.
Gass.
        p.   cm. — (PAJ books)
    ISBN 0-8018-5133-5 (pbk. : acid-free)
    I. Title.   II. Title: Relation of human nature to the human mind.
III. Series.
PS3537.T323G37   1995
812'.52—dc20   94-46361
                                                                  CIP

Printed in the United States
3900

9 780801 851339